With her aircraft ranged for flying operations, *Glory* steams at speed through a calm sea.

HMS Glory
1945-1961

Neil McCart

In Association with the

FLEET AIR ARM
MUSEUM

Printed and bound in Italy by
Fotolito Longo

Contents

Foreword

by
"Spiv" Leahy

HMS GLORY, her name has a ring to it, it is a proud name and it was easy for her ships company to be proud of her.

By the time I joined GLORY in mid 1952 she was, by then, nearly two thirds of the way through what was to be a relatively short, if eventful, life. Our squadron worked up with the ship in the Mediterranean prior to the ship returning to Korea for her third tour of operations.

Whenever a squadron joins a particular carrier for the first time there is always some concern as to how the squadron will fit in with the ship. It is possible for a "them" and "us" attitude to develop which makes life more difficult for all parties than it need to be. This is not surprising as the need of the Air Department to carry out flying operations is not necessarily in line with the ship's requirements. Even the simple task of going from A to B is made more difficult if the ship has repeatedly to turn around and go full speed in the opposite direction from its preferred course in order to launch and recover aircraft. We soon found out that we need not have worried as in GLORY we were soon made to feel that we were all of one company.

During our time conducting operations off Korea, in often appalling weather during the winter, the ship retained her reputation as a happy ship despite the casualties that were suffered. GLORY also consistently achieved an intensity of operations not previously reached by a British carrier. The pattern of operations undoubtedly helped achieve this but, more importantly, without the hard work by all hands this standard would never have been reached.

GLORY and others in the Colossus class of light fleet carriers were in their time an ideal match of aircraft and their carriers. A match which was not always to be seen in later years as more capable and larger jet aircraft came along and had to be shoehorned even into the larger Fleet carriers.

I am pleased that this book has been produced and believe it will be appreciated by those who served in GLORY and it will serve for others as an accurate and interesting record of life as it was in a Royal Navy Light Fleet carrier some fifty years ago.

PER CONCORDIAM GLORIA

"Spiv" Leahy was a Sea Fury pilot in *Glory* at the time of the Korean war - serving in 804 Naval Air Squadron. He was awarded the DSC after the war. He went on to serve as a test pilot for the Buccaneer jet before it entered naval service. He eventually retired as a Captain RN.

Chapter One

A New Light Fleet Aircraft Carrier
August 1942 - April 1945

When the Second World War broke out on 3 September 1939, the Royal Navy had only seven aircraft carriers and of those just one, *Ark Royal*, could be said to be modern. Only she and the small, obsolete *Hermes* had been specifically designed as aircraft carriers, with *Argus* and *Eagle* having been converted from a merchant ship hull and from the hull of what was to have been a battleship for the Chilean Navy respectively. The other three, *Furious*, *Glorious* and *Courageous*, had all been converted from light battlecruisers in the 1920s.

During the pre-war years the Fleet Air Arm was controlled by the Royal Air Force, and consequently it had not been give a high priority as resources were used to build up the RAF's bomber force. In 1937, when the Admiralty gained full control of the Fleet Air Arm, an expansion programme was initiated, but it could not be completed before war came in 1939. Only 14 days after the declaration of war the fleet carrier *Courageous* was sunk by a U-boat whilst carrying out an anti-submarine patrol in the South West Approaches. Nine months later, in June 1940, her sister ship *Glorious* was sunk by gunfire from the German battlecruisers *Scharnhorst* and *Gneisenau* during the Allied withdrawal from Norway. At this early stage of the war the battleship still reigned supreme as the Navy's capital ship.

Fortunately, it had been recognized that air power at sea was vital to the fleet, and in April 1937 the keel had been laid for the first of six large 23,000-ton fleet aircraft carriers. However, with their heavily armoured flight decks and hangars, and their medium calibre guns, each ship would take over three years to build and it would be 1944 before the final two, *Implacable* and *Indefatigable*, were commissioned. As the Second World War progressed the vital importance of air power at sea became ever more apparent. In November 1940, 21 Swordfish aircraft from *Illustrious* attacked the Italian naval base at Taranto, and for the loss of only two aircraft, three enemy battleships were crippled. Six months later it was aircraft from *Ark Royal* that disabled the German battleship *Bismarck*, allowing units of the Home Fleet to then catch and sink her. Without the Fleet Air Arm it is likely that this mighty battleship would have reached the safety of north-western France.

Later that year, on 7 December 1941, carrier-borne aircraft of the Imperial Japanese Navy delivered a devastating blow to the US Navy's Pacific Fleet at Pearl Harbour, when they sank four battleships and seriously damaged others. Significantly, however, the American carrier fleet was at sea on exercises and escaped unscathed to play what would be a major role in the Pacific War. Just three days later, on a calm and sunny day in the South China Sea, one hundred torpedo bombers of the Japanese Navy's First Air Group, based at Saigon, sank the battleship *Prince of Wales* and the elderly battlecruiser *Repulse*. The Japanese lost only four aircraft, and the action dramatically ended the dominant role of the battleship in modern naval warfare.

As a result, in early 1942 it was decided to design a new class of aircraft carrier, which was capable of a speed of 25 knots and which would carry at least 35 to 40 fighter aircraft. The basic design work was entrusted to Vickers Armstrong Shipbuilders, who had experience of both merchant ship and warship construction, for it had been decided that the new carriers would be built largely to merchant ship standards. This would allow the vessels to be constructed quickly and it would also enable more shipbuilding companies to tender for contracts. In the event, to expedite the completion of the ships it had been decided to limit the defensive armament to anti-aircraft weapons and, apart from splinter protection for torpedo warheads, they were to have no conventional armour. Instead there would be a complete sub-division of the main machinery compartments and the steering gear. It was also decided that the operational life of these new carriers would be limited to just three years, or until the end of the war which, at that time, could not be foreseen. With a displacement tonnage of just over

Lady Cynthia Brooke, the wife of Northern Ireland's Prime Minister, breaks a bottle of Empire wine on *Glory's* bow as she names the ship.

The workers at Harland & Wolff's Belfast shipyard rush across the slipway as *Glory* slides towards the waters of the River Lagan.

13,000 tons, an overall length of 695 feet and beam of 112 feet, the vessels would give the appearance of being smaller versions of the Illustrious-class fleet aircraft carriers. Initially there were to be eight ships which, named after the first to be laid down, would become the Colossus class. They were to be some of the Royal Navy's most successful warships.

The keel of the name ship was laid on 1 June 1942, and two months later, on Thursday 27 August, at the Belfast shipyard of Harland & Wolff Ltd, the keel plates were laid for the second vessel of the class, which would eventually become *Glory*. Building work on the carrier's hull progressed quickly, and in the late autumn of the following year the first naval personnel, under the command of Commander (E) W. J. Henton-Jones RNR, travelled to Belfast to stand by during the later stages of building and fitting out. By late November 1943 the hull was ready for launching. The ceremony was carried out by Lady Cynthia Brooke, the wife of Sir Basil Brooke, who was both the Minister of Commerce and the Prime Minister of Northern Ireland. With strict press censorship in force the event went largely unnoticed, but in the shipyard itself the officers and men who were standing by the ship gathered by the launch platform and beneath the bows of the ship. As always on such occasions all work in the shipyard stopped, and the whole work-force gathered round the slipway to witness this important event for the city of Belfast. At midday on Saturday 27 November 1943, Lady Brooke released the trigger which, in its turn, smashed a bottle of Empire wine against *Glory's* stem and sent the ship down the slipway into the Musgrave Channel, from where she was towed quickly round to the nearby Thompson Wharf where fitting out could begin.

Glory's twin screws were powered by two sets of Parsons geared steam turbines, in two engine rooms, which developed 40,000 SHP and gave her a speed of 25 knots. The superheated steam for the turbines was provided by four Admiralty Three Drum boilers in two boiler rooms. She could carry some 3,196 tons of furnace fuel oil. Her defensive armament was limited to, 2 pdr pom-poms in four six barrelled mountings. Her single hangar was 332 feet long, which included a 57ft extension aft of the after lift. Two aircraft lifts 45 feet long and 35 feet wide, were installed forward and aft, and she was able to carry some 40 aircraft. She was also fitted with one hydraulic accelerator

On 21 February 1945, after travelling to Belfast by special trains and ferry, the main body of the ship's company arrived on board. In this photograph the first drafts carry their kitbags over the brow.

(catapult) which was capable of launching a 16,000lb aircraft at 66 knots. Despite the austere design of the Colossus-class carriers they were equipped with better radar than the fleet carriers, and had almost double the aviation fuel stowage. Their flight decks and hangars were almost the same size as those found on the fleet carriers, and with their simple machinery they would prove to be far more economical to run. So successful was the design that the first eight ships of the Colossus class were quickly followed by six slightly improved versions known as the Majestic class. In the event, however, none of the latter class were completed before the end of the war and none of them saw service with the Royal Navy.

On 1 November 1944, *Glory's* first commanding officer, Captain Sir Anthony W. Buzzard DSO OBE RN, joined the ship at Belfast. On Wednesday 21 February 1945, *Glory* was inspected by the Admiral

The first aircraft to arrive on board at Belfast were three Vought Corsairs. Here one of the machines, together with crates of stores and equipment, waits to be loaded aboard.

Superintendent, Contract Built Ships, and at midday she was commissioned by the officers and men who were standing by her. That same afternoon, having been issued with commissioning cards and mess traps, the main body of the ship's company arrived in Belfast by ferry and special trains to join their ship. At 1600 that day watchkeeping duties were started and 24 hours later further drafts, together with all their kit, were embarked.

Within 24 hours of the ship's company joining *Glory* the long process of embarking stores and ammunition got under way. On Tuesday 27 February the first aircraft, in the form of three Vought F3 Corsairs, were hoisted on board, having been towed alongside by tractors. In early March the ship was opened to Harland & Wolff's foremen and their wives and two days later, on 6 March, Captain Dallmeyer,

the commanding officer of *Glory's* sister ship *Venerable*, paid her a visit. *Venerable*, which had been launched on 30 December 1943, a month after *Glory*, was undergoing her initial flying trials and was anchored in Belfast Lough that day. As *Glory* neared completion the ship was opened to the public and Belfast residents flocked to see the latest warship to be built in their city. During this period there was no shortage of VIP visitors, with the Flag Officer Northern Ireland, two Army generals and the ship's sponsor, Lady Brooke, looking round the carrier. Sir Basil and Lady Brooke arrived on board during the afternoon of Monday 19 March, and before she left Lady Brooke addressed the ship's company over the tannoy and wished them luck for the future.

Although there was still some hard fighting to come, the Allied armies in Europe had occupied large

Glory at sea soon after leaving Harland & Wolff's shipyard. Her hull painted in the British Pacific Fleet's camouflage colours.

An Avenger "lands on" during *Glory's* initial flying trials in the Firth of Clyde.

First hiccup......A Barracuda of 837 Squadron is damaged whilst landing on during *Glory's* initial trials and work-up.

On a wet and windy day in the Firth of Clyde, "Jumbo", the flight deck crane, moves in to shift another damaged Barracuda.

areas of Germany and the end of the war in Europe was at last in sight. In the Far East and the Pacific theatres of war, however, the hostilities appeared to be far from over, with the Japanese putting up fierce resistance as the US-led advance moved ever closer to the Japanese mainland. In the Pacific War the aircraft carrier was, without doubt, the main weapon in the Allies' arsenal, and the British Pacific Fleet was soon to be in the forefront of operations against the Japanese. As part of the build-up in the Pacific it had been decided to form the 11th Aircraft Carrier Squadron, which would comprise *Indomitable* and the first four new Colossus-class light fleet carriers, *Colossus*, *Glory*, *Venerable* and *Vengeance*. With the battleship *Anson*, the cruisers *Bermuda* and *Swiftsure*, and the destroyers *Kempenfelt*, *Tumult*, *Tuscan*, *Tyrian*, *Ursa* and *Whirlwind*, they were to form Task Group 111.2 of the British Pacific Fleet. After their arrival at Sydney it was planned that they would become operational on 20 August 1945.

Four days after the visit of her sponsor, at 0807 on Friday 23 March 1945, *Glory* slipped her mooring

ropes at the Thompson Wharf and, looking resplendent in her Pacific camouflage paint scheme, she moved slowly down the River Lagan, into Belfast Lough and Bangor Bay to start her initial trials. Next day, escorted by the elderly destroyer, *Westcott*, she steamed across to the Firth of Clyde for two days of full-power trials and timed runs off the Skelmorlie measured mile. Each afternoon she would anchor off Greenock which provided the ship's company with a change from Belfast as an evening run ashore. During the early afternoon of Friday 30 March, with the carrier in the Firth of Clyde, "Flying Stations" was piped and at 1312 the first deck landing was made by a Seafire. During the rest of the afternoon three Seafires and the three Corsairs which had been embarked at Belfast made a series of deck landings and launchings from the accelerator. Finally, after a busy day of flying trials, *Glory* anchored off Greenock for the weekend.

When flying trials resumed on Monday 2 April, the three Corsairs were flown off and during the next day the Barracudas of 837 Squadron landed on to carry out two weeks of flying practice. On Tuesday 10 April there was a break in the flying routine when a Swordfish aircraft, carrying two Army officers as passengers, landed on. With *Lancaster Castle* acting as her escort, *Glory* continued her intensive flying practice in the Firth of Clyde, anchoring each evening off either Lamlash or Greenock. At 1005 on Wednesday 18 April came the first fatal aircraft accident. *Glory* had left her Greenock anchorage at 0847 that forenoon and as the Barracudas were being ranged to start the day's flying, two aircraft handlers were slow to react and they were caught by the blades of a propeller. One man, Able Seaman Emerson, was killed outright and the second, Able Seaman Mason, was seriously injured. With flying temporarily halted the ship steamed in close to Largs Pier where the injured man was rushed to hospital and the body of AB Emerson was landed for burial.

That evening, when the ship anchored off Greenock, there was an 18-day break, with leave being given to both watches before the final preparations were made to embark her two squadrons, with all their personnel and stores. She would then be ready to complete her work-up in the Eastern Mediterranean and take her place as part of the British Pacific Fleet for the final stages of the war against Japan.

Chapter Two

The Surrender of Japan:
May - September 1945

Carrying an additional deck cargo of aircraft *Glory* steams east to join the British Pacific Fleet.

During the afternoon of Sunday 6 May 1945 *Glory* sailed from Greenock. Later that day she landed on three Barracudas, three Firebrands and a Wildcat, all seven of which remained with her for two days carrying out an intensive programme of flying practice. During the early evening of 7 May, with the aircraft having flown ashore, she anchored off Greenock once again, where the personnel of 837 Squadron were embarked, and where the ship's company were able to enjoy the VE Day celebrations. Four days later, having embarked the River Clyde pilot, *Glory* weighed anchor and steamed upriver to secure alongside King George V Dock, just off Govan's Renfrew Road, and close to RNAS Abbotsinch (now Glasgow International Airport). During her three days alongside the personnel of 1831

(Corsair) Squadron were embarked, as well as stores and equipment. Here the ship's company had the luxury of being able to get ashore without relying on liberty boats, but they were to be the last UK runs ashore that they would enjoy for 16 months.

After her long weekend alongside in Govan, *Glory* left the River Clyde during the afternoon of Monday 14 May and, together with the destroyers *Hotspur* and *Icarus*, she set course for the Mediterranean. During the passage she embarked the Corsairs of 1831 Squadron and the Barracudas of 837 Squadron, and anti-aircraft exercises were carried out with her own Corsairs providing the attacking force. Four days after leaving the Clyde she arrived off Gibraltar, where she anchored in the Bay just long enough to embark and land mail, before setting course for Malta. Two days

During the afternoon of 21 May 1945, whilst *Glory* was at anchor off Malta, Rear-Admiral Harcourt, Flag Officer 11th Aircraft Carrier Squadron, who was flying his flag in *Venerable*, visited *Glory*. Here he is being piped aboard and being greeted by Captain Buzzard.

into the passage she passed the Italian cruiser *Pompeo Magno*, which was one of the few modern Italian naval units to have survived the war in Europe. On the following day, Monday 21 May, she joined her sister ship *Vengeance* (Captain D. M. L. Neame RN) at anchor in Marsaxlokk Bay (Malta). Later that afternoon she was joined by *Venerable* (Captain W. A. Dallmeyer RN), flying the flag of Rear-Admiral C. H. J. Harcourt, Flag Officer 11th Aircraft Carrier Squadron. The fourth carrier of the squadron, *Colossus* (Captain G. H. Stokes CB DSO RN) was at Alexandria.

That same afternoon Rear-Admiral Harcourt paid a three-hour visit to *Glory*, with the Royal Marines providing an extremely smart guard and band. The three carriers did not stay long off Malta and early on the morning of 22 May they weighed anchor and set course for Alexandria. Shortly after sailing *Glory* experienced her first aircraft loss, when a Corsair crashed into the sea following an accelerated take-off. Fortunately, the pilot was recovered safely and all three carriers were able to practise joint flying exercises as they steamed south-east. On 24 May they arrived at Alexandria, where they joined *Colossus*, moored to buoys in the harbour. Once *Glory* was safely secured, the task of disembarking squadron personnel and stores began, for she was to undergo an essen-

tial maintenance period. Five days later she put to sea for just 24 hours in order to fly the aircraft ashore, after which she returned to harbour and nine days later she was lifted out of the water, spending five days in the Admiralty Floating Dry Dock which was based in the Egyptian port. It was the first opportunity since leaving Harland & Wolff's yard at Belfast for work to be carried out on the underwater hull, which was thoroughly scraped and repainted. Seven days later, on Saturday 16 June, when she moved back to her buoy in the harbour, she was the only aircraft carrier present as her three sisters had all sailed for Trincomalee. On the following Monday she was ready to complete her work-up and she set sail with the cruiser *Cleopatra*.

Each day until the end of June *Glory* would leave harbour during the morning or forenoon watch and squadrons would carry out ten hours of intensive flying practice, before the ship returned to Alexandria's outer harbour each evening. Finally, during the afternoon of Friday 29 June the Flag Officer Eastern Mediterranean carried out both sea and harbour inspections of the ship, and there was one last run ashore at the Egyptian port. During the evening of Sunday 1 July *Glory*, escorted by the destroyer *Wizard*, left Alexandria and set course east for Port Said. Both ships made their southbound transits of the

Glory at sea during her work-up in the Eastern Mediterranean. Barracudas of 837 Squadron and Corsairs of 1831 Squadron are on deck.

11

Suez Canal during 3 July, and by 1830 that day they were steaming south through the Gulf of Suez. With the other three carriers having arrived at Tricomalee in mid-June, both *Glory* and *Wizard* made their best speed across the Arabian Sea and Indian Ocean, pausing only for *Glory* to refuel the destroyer. The passage took just nine days, and during the early evening of 16 July they secured to buoys in Trincomalee's picturesque natural harbour. With *Venerable* and *Vengeance* having just left for Madras, and *Colossus* in Colombo, the only other aircraft carriers in harbour at the time were the escort carriers *Empress* and *Shah*.

As *Glory* was due in Sydney by mid-August there was little free time for the ship's company and it was not long before she and *Wizard* were at sea and involved in intensive exercises. They practised night encounter exercises, the Corsairs bombed splash targets, and the Barracudas exercised attacks on both *Glory* and *Wizard*. Kamikaze attacks had taken a heavy toll on Allied ships in the Pacific, and counter measures were exercised regularly. There was a five-day visit to Colombo, which proved to be a livelier and more popular run ashore than Trincomalee. Finally however, at 1045 on Friday 3 August *Glory*, together with her faithful escort *Wizard*, left Colombo for a fast passage across the Indian Ocean, bound for Fremantle. There was time though to carry out the Crossing the Line ceremony, with Neptune and his Court being piped on board one evening and appearing on the forward lift. Here King Neptune presented Captain Buzzard with a list of those who were earmarked for a ducking. Next day the Royal Marines Detachment did a splendid job of catching and depositing the victims, including the Captain himself, into a makeshift swimming pool on the flight deck. Three days into the passage, on 6 August, the United States Air Force B-29 bomber, *Enola Gay*, dropped the first atomic bomb on the city of Hiroshima and three days after that, on 9 August, a second atomic bomb was dropped on Nagasaki. On the following day *Glory* and *Wizard* arrived in Fremantle, where they went alongside for a short 20-hour stopover at the West Australian port.

Although the news of the "new type of bomb" which had been dropped on the two Japanese cities came through to the ship in news bulletins, the full significance of the way they had dramatically altered the course of the war in the Pacific and South-East Asia was not appreciated, and as far as *Glory*'s ship's company were concerned they were still on course to undertake operations in the Pacific. After an unforgettable run ashore in Fremantle, when *Glory* and *Wizard* left the Western Australian port on Saturday 11 August there were more than a few hangovers on board. Once again the two ships were ordered to make their best speed, this time for Sydney. There then followed a fast passage across the Great Australian Bight so that by the morning of Wednesday 15 August they were just 24 hours steaming away from Sydney Heads. At 0835 there came the welcome sight of one of *Anson*'s aircraft as it rendezvoused with the two ships and circled overhead, but less than half an hour later, at 0900, came the even more welcome news over the ships' tannoys that Japan had agreed to surrender - which meant that the Second World War was finally over. Next morning the squadrons were flown off to RANAS Nowra, and at 1000 *Glory* secured alongside No 3 wharf Woolloomooloo Docks, Sydney. *Glory*'s ship's company then spent the last two weeks of August enjoying the lavish hospitality of the people of Sydney with each watch being granted several days leave. Understandably, Captain Buzzard's offer was taken up with gusto by everyone on board. The ships of the Pacific Fleet were welcomed back into Sydney with sirens and hooters as the Australian people expressed their gratitude. During the afternoon of Sunday 26 August there was an opportunity for the ship's company to repay this generous treatment when *Glory* was opened to visitors. By the following week, however, it was clear that the sojourn was coming to an end when the carrier was ordered to prepare for sea.

The end of the war against Japan had come more quickly then expected, and all over the Pacific and South-East Asia Japanese armies, which had not been defeated on the field of battle, still occupied vast areas and controlled thousands of Allied prisoners of war. It was known that the latter had suffered terribly at the hands of their captors and initially Allied efforts would be directed towards liberating and repatriating all these POWs. On 29 August the first force of US troops arrived at Yokohama, and on the following day an American airborne division landed at the Yokosuka naval base. That same day, in Tokyo Bay, Allied warships began to gather, including the battleships *USS Missouri* and *HMS Duke of York*, to prepare for the

At 1105 on Thursday 6 September 1945, with *Glory* having stopped off the coast of Rabaul, Japanese delegates arrived on board to surrender all their Army and Naval Forces in their South-Eastern area of operations. In this photograph they are still wet from a choppy boat ride out to the ship.

main surrender ceremony on 2 September which would be presided over by General Douglas MacArthur. On 30 August, a British naval squadron, which would soon be joined by *Glory's* sister ship *Vengeance*, arrived in Hong Kong, and the first British Army units were parachuted into Changi prisoner of war camp in Singapore.

During the first week of September, Japanese garrisons throughout South-East Asia and the Pacific were surrendering to Allied forces, and the evacuation of ex-prisoners of war was started. At this time the Australian Government requested the assistance of the Royal Navy to help with the surrender of the Japanese army and naval units occupying the islands of New Britain, Bougainville, New Ireland and its adjacent islands. The 1st Australian Army, fighting the campaign in New Guinea in the steaming rainforests over the Kokoda Trail, right across the Owen Stanley Range of mountains, had endured appalling conditions. It was fitting, therefore, that the Commander of the 1st Army, Lt-General V. A. H. Sturdee, should take the surrender of Japanese forces in the South-Eastern Area.

At 0800 on Saturday 1 September General Sturdee

embarked, and three-quarters of an hour later the *Glory's* mooring ropes were slipped and she left the harbour to embark her squadrons. Once this had been completed she set course for Jacquinot Bay on the south side of the island of New Britain, accompanied by her escorts, HM Ships *Amethyst* and *Hart*. Because it was not known how individual Japanese garrisons would react to the news of their country's surrender and to guard against last-ditch suicide attacks Beaufort aircraft from the Royal Australian Air Force provided air cover for the force during the passage. As *Glory* and her escorts neared their immediate destination, anti-aircraft guns were manned and the ship went to the third degree of readiness, before eventually anchoring well offshore, in Jacquinot Bay, during the forenoon of Wednesday 5 September. That afternoon General Sturdee went ashore to organize surrender parties, who returned to the ship with him. At 1755 *Glory* and the two sloops weighed anchor to make an overnight passage through St George's Channel to Rabaul on the north of the island. Next morning, at 0750, with all gun crews closed up at "Action Stations", and with *Amethyst* and *Hart* stationed one mile on either side of the carrier, *Glory* arrived off

Lieutenant-General Imamura surrenders his ceremonial sword to Lieutenant-General V. A. H. Sturdee, General Officer Commanding the 1st Australian Army. Members of the ship's company behind the table are still wearing their No8-working rig.

Rabaul. It had been decided that, in case of an enemy attack, she would not anchor, so instead, the main engines were stopped, with the engine rooms remaining at immediate notice for steam, and she drifted offshore. There were a few worrying moments when, soon after stopping, an unusual vibration was felt throughout the ship, but it was soon realized that this was caused by an earthquake in the area. Clearly the forces of nature had no sense of occasion that day.

At 1040 the duty watch was placed at a third degree of readiness, and all those members of the ship's company who were off watch were ordered to fall in on the flight deck by divisions. Twenty-five minutes later the Japanese military officers of the surrender delegation, led by Lt-General H. Imamura and Vice-Admiral K. Kusaka, arrived on board, their uniforms still wet, after what had been a choppy boat ride from Rabaul. After preliminary discussions below decks about the Japanese military installations ashore, at 1130, with

the ship stopped in a position Lat 04°-32'S/Long 152°-34'E, Lt-General Imamura, Vice-Admiral Kusaka and their delegation were marched under escort along the flight deck, in front of the assembled ship's company, to a small table covered by green baize on which were arranged the surrender document, pens and ink. Behind which stood General Sturdee and his staff. After first laying down their ceremonial swords as a symbol of surrender, both senior Japanese officers signed the document surrendering the Japanese South-Eastern Army and the naval forces in the area. As soon as this had been completed the whole delegation was again escorted below decks for further talks on the military dispositions in the area. While these talks were under way *Glory* and her escorts steamed slowly at ten knots off the northern coast of New Britain. Finally, shortly before 1500, with the surrender complete, the ship stopped close to Rabaul and both the Japanese and Allied delegations were disembarked by boat to *Hart*, after which *Glory* set course back to Sydney.

With flying exercises being carried out, the return passage took six days and it was during the late forenoon of Wednesday 12 September that *Glory's* squadrons were flown off. A few hours later she entered Sydney Harbour and secured to a buoy.

Having arrived in the Pacific too late to take an active part in operations against Japan, the ship had played an important role in the surrender of the Japanese South-Eastern Army and Navy. Now, whilst the dockyard took over *Glory* to prepare her for duty as a repatriation ship, her ship's company could relax once again and enjoy 14 days in Australia's largest city.

A plaque commemorating the surrender was subsequently fitted to *Glory's* flight deck.

Chapter Three

Missions of Mercy
September - December 1945

After the Japanese surrender, the next major task for the Allied forces was to rescue and repatriate all the Allied prisoners of war who had been held in prison camps all over South-East Asia. It was well known that ill-treatment and neglect had taken its toll on them, and it was imperative that the rescue operation was carried out quickly and efficiently. The Royal Navy had already committed ships of the Pacific Fleet to the task and on 25 September 1945, the fleet carrier *Implacable*, with over 2,000 ex-POWs embarked, had left Manila bound for Pearl

Harbour and Vancouver.

Meanwhile, during her 13-day stay in Sydney in the second half of September, dockyard workers swarmed over *Glory* as the ship was fitted out to carry former prisoners of war on the first stage of their voyage home. In the main hangar 200 beds were set up, with a complete mobile hospital at the after end. The forward hangar was fitted out as a dining hall and recreation centre, with refectory tables and benches. In the forward lift well a mobile cinema, complete with twin projectors and a full size screen, was set up. With the

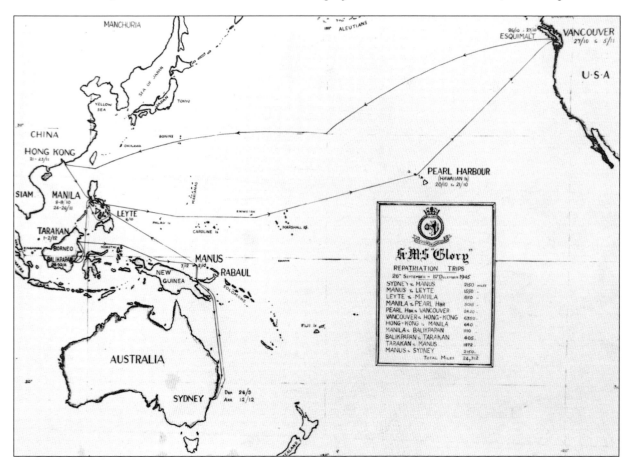

Having taken the Japanese surrender of their South-Eastern area of occupation, *Glory's* next task was to assist with the repatriation of Allied prisoners of war and internees. This chart shows the voyages made between 26 September and 12 December 1945.

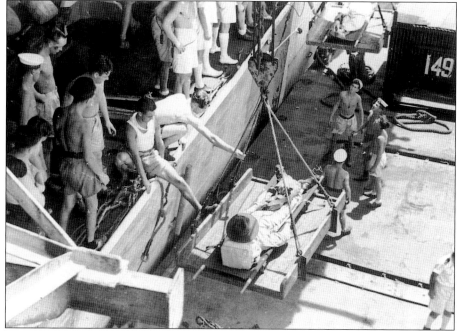

After years of neglect and abuse many Allied prisoners of war were in poor physical condition and were unable to walk. These men were hoisted on board on stretchers.

squadrons ashore their mess decks were emptied and prepared for the new passengers, with some cabins in the wardroom flat being reserved for 36 nursing sisters who had volunteered to join the ship for this mercy mission.

When *Glory* left Sydney during the afternoon of Wednesday 26 September, she was initially ordered to the Pacific Fleet base at Manus in the Admiralty Islands. After refuelling there she was ordered to Leyte Gulf in the southern Philippines, where she arrived during the forenoon of 6 October. After only a brief stay she left for Manila Bay later in the day. On leaving Sydney the ship's company had got together to organize evening games and PT to amuse the passengers, and the Royal Marines Detachment trained for a boxing tournament. During the passage, with fine weather and calm seas, the ship's company themselves had 15 minutes of PT each afternoon. However, when Captain Gosling RM tried to recruit volunteers for his boxing teams, he found many who had boasted of once being champs of the Mediterranean, Home or China Fleets, suddenly developed "old complaints", which prevented them from taking part.

Glory anchored in Manila Bay at 0837 on Monday 8 October, and during the remainder of that day lighters came alongside with large loads of new Army

uniforms for the passengers, which had to be embarked and sorted. Next day, at 0900, the first relay of landing craft came alongside with the initial batch of passengers who were all serious hospital cases. Over 1,100, mainly British, ex-POWs were embarked, including five Royal Marines who were survivors from the sinking of *Prince of Wales* and *Repulse*. Following the loss of the two capital ships the marines had been attached to Army units, and had been taken prisoner on 15 February 1942 when the garrison at Singapore surrendered to the Japanese. It was not long before the improvised hospital in the hangar was full of men who, after years of ill treatment and near-starvation, were literally walking skeletons. Finally, at 1824 on Tuesday 9 October, with the embarkation complete, *Glory* weighed anchor and set course for Pearl Harbour.

Fortunately, the sea was calm for the Pacific voyage, which enabled the officers and men, from Captain Buzzard downwards, to carry out their well-planned programme of sports and amusements for the passengers. Deck hockey and "horse racing" proved to be particular favourites, with the cinema, improvised concerts and tombola heading the list of favourite evening pastimes. Sadly, at 0550 on Monday 15 October, six days out from Manila, Sapper William Owers, Royal Engineers, died from

During *Glory's* 13-day stay in Sydney in late September 1945, the main hangar was fitted with 200 beds and a complete mobile hospital. It was known that ill-treatment had taken its toll on the prisoners of war. In this photograph patients are seen occupying the beds during their repatriation voyage.

tuberculosis. That evening, in a position Lat 11°-32'N/Long 163°-05'E, at a funeral service which was attended by large numbers of both ship's company and passengers, his body was committed to the deep. Sapper Owers, like most of the passengers, had been captured at the fall of Singapore and his loss, when he was so close to going home, affected everyone deeply. Two days later, on Wednesday 17 October, the International Date Line was crossed which meant that day was repeated. At 0515 on Saturday 20 October land was sighted on the starboard beam as *Glory* approached the main Hawaiian island of Oahu. Later

During her repatriation voyages 36 nursing sisters were embarked in *Glory*. Here one of them tends her patients.

With so many ex-prisoners of war on board, *Glory's* forward hangar was fitted out as a dining hall and recreation centre. This photograph shows the improvised dining facilities in use by the ex-POWs.

that forenoon she berthed at the Ford Island Naval Base at Pearl Harbour, and leave was granted to the ship's company and those passengers who were fit enough to venture ashore. The main reason for the stopover was to enable the carrier to refuel, so in the short time available few got beyond the main US Navy canteen, but everyone who did go ashore was made very welcome by the American servicemen. A few even made it to Waikiki Beach. After less than 24 hours alongside *Glory* left Pearl Harbour, and no sooner had the golden Hawaiian beaches slipped over the horizon than the air temperatures got noticeably cooler and the ship's company changed into their blue uniforms. By this time most of the passengers had lost their "haunted" look and were fit enough to join in even the most boisterous games of deck hockey. More surprisingly still, according to one member of the ship's company: "Even the nurses were allowed to wander from the "holy ground" they occupied in the wardroom flat back aft, and they enjoyed themselves too."

The Pacific voyage came to an end on Friday 26 October when, at 0900, *Glory* approached the small Canadian naval base of Esquimalt, close to Vancouver. Naturally there was great excitement on board the carrier as she steamed into the harbour amidst the cacophony of sound from sirens, bells,

hooters, car horns and anything else which made a noise. So enthusiastic was the welcome that the Royal Marines Band on the flight deck, were drowned out by two rather loud bands on the jetty. By 1035 *Glory's* mooring lines had been secured, but disembarkation did not begin at once and the passengers were able to enjoy one last meal aboard their temporary home. That afternoon the lower deck was cleared and the Officer Commanding the troops presented an inscribed silver bugle and a mace to the ship, as a token of thanks for the way the ship's company had looked after them during their first weeks of freedom. Captain Buzzard replied with a few words on behalf of all on board the carrier and after three hearty cheers from both the ship's company and passengers, disembarkation got under way.

Many of *Glory's* officers and men had become good friends with the passengers. Five Royal Marines who had survived the sinking of their ships, the last bloody battles in southern Malaya and the final defensive perimeter around Singapore City, followed by three and a half years of cruel imprisonment, had been taken under the protective wing of Captain Gosling, Officer Commanding Royal Marines, and his detachment. However, all the passengers were eager to start the next stage of their long journey home, and they were soon moving down the gangway to board the

At the end of her repatriation voyage, *Glory* spent nine days in Vancouver, Canada. The local people are clearly interested in the carrier as she lies alongside.

seemingly endless rows of buses that were waiting for them on the jetty. That evening the ship's hangar was deserted, and the ship's company were enjoying a run ashore in the small town of Esquimalt. Next morning *Glory* slipped her mooring ropes to complete her passage of the Juan de Fuca Strait, before steaming north through the Strait of Georgia and under Lion's Gate Bridge to berth alongside in Vancouver City itself.

For nine days the ship's company enjoyed the hospitality of the Canadian city, but all too soon the visit came to an end, and after the goodbyes to a lot of new-found friends, *Glory* sailed on the morning of Monday 5 November. With Vancouver having faded into the distance astern, course was set for Hong Kong. For this return crossing of the Pacific Ocean, however, the weather was not kind and for the first few days few people ventured up onto the flight deck. The nurses now had little to do during the 16-day non-stop voy-

age before *Glory* arrived in Hong Kong Harbour during the forenoon of Wednesday 21 November, having missed 13 November altogether when she again crossed the International Date Line. With the colony only recently having been reoccupied by British forces, leave was limited to afternoons and evenings until 2230. However, with both Hong Kong Island and Kowloon still recovering from the privations of the Japanese occupation, the dance halls of Wanchai were unusually quiet. After just 48 hours in Hong Kong, *Glory* was ordered to Manila Bay and after a 36-hour passage anchored off the Philippine City at 1830. Once again she was to repatriate ex-prisoners of the Japanese, but this time they were Dutch civilian internees, including women and children.

Having embarked her passengers *Glory* left Manila Bay, but this time she made only a short, two-day, passage to Balikpapen on the south-east coast of Borneo in what was then the Dutch East Indies. On arrival in the harbour she was able to go alongside, but this time Japanese prisoners of war, in a reversal of roles, provided the working parties to land all the passengers' baggage. Their working conditions were, it must be said, far better than those which they had inflicted on their prisoners. During the two days the carrier was alongside, because of the threat of civil unrest ashore and opposition to the returning Dutch colonial authorities, leave was severely restricted. On her departure from Balikpapen *Glory* made a short overnight passage north to the island of Tarakan, where she anchored offshore.

Rumours were circulating round the ship that Christmas was to be spent in Sydney, and at Tarakan the "buzzes" appeared to be confirmed when troops of the Australian 7th Division, who had been involved in some of the heaviest fighting against the Japanese in Borneo, were embarked for the passage home. After spending two days embarking the troops and their equipment, at 1615 on 2 December *Glory* weighed anchor and left Tarakan, bound for Manus. After a five-day passage there was a short break at the Admiralty Islands base before the carrier resumed her voyage to Sydney. Five days later, during the morning watch of Wednesday 12 December, she arrived off Sydney Heads where she was met by the Australian destroyer *Queenborough* for the final passage up harbour. Three hours later the pilot was embarked and *Glory* steamed through Sydney Harbour where the troops received a tumultuous welcome. At 0955 she secured alongside No 7 berth at Woolloomooloo Docks where her passengers were disembarked. The ship's company could now look forward to a four-week break as *Glory* underwent a maintenance period, during which her temporary passenger accommodation was removed and she was refitted to resume her role as an operational aircraft carrier.

Flagship in the Far East
January 1946 - October 1947

For the officers and men of *Glory* the Christmas and New Year of 1945-46 were, perhaps, the most memorable few weeks of the commission. They were able to enjoy the surfing beaches at Manly and Bondi, the ice-cold lager and the traditional Christmas Dinner and New Year festivities. On the last day of December 1945, *Glory's* sister ship *Venerable* arrived in Sydney from Trincomalee, just in time to see in the New Year. On Wednesday 9 January 1946 *Glory* was towed down harbour to the Captain Cook dry dock on Garden Island, where she remained for five days. During this time essential maintenance was carried out on the underwater hull.

On 15 January, however, she was ready for sea again and at 0920 that day she left harbour and set course for Jervis Bay.

During the afternoon of 15 January the Corsairs of 1831 Squadron and the Fireflies of 837 Squadron, which had replaced the Barracudas, landed on safely. For four days, together with the destroyers *Armada* and *Tumult*, and the fleet carrier *Implacable*, *Glory* exercised in the Jervis Bay area. On 20 January she returned to Sydney, but only to wait in the outer harbour for just over three hours, for at midday she weighed anchor to leave in formation with the fleet carriers *Implacable* and *Indefatigable* (Flag Vice-

During the forenoon of 23 January 1946, with her ship's company manning the flight deck and Corsairs and Fireflies ranged, *Glory* enters Melbourne for the Royal Navy's first visit to the port since before the start of the Second World War.

For the visit to Melbourne *Glory* was in company with the fleet carriers *Indefatigable* and *Implacable*. This aerial photograph shows the three carriers secured alongside Station Pier. *Glory* is moored forward of *Implacable*.

Admiral Sir Philip Vian), and the destroyers *Armada* and *Tuscan*. The squadron was bound for Melbourne to show the flag in the State Capital of Victoria, which had not seen any major Royal Navy ships since the outbreak of war in September 1939. During the three-day passage *Glory's* squadrons carried out joint flying operations with the two fleet carriers, and in the early hours of Wednesday 23 January, the force arrived off the mouth of the Yarra River. At just before 0600 pilots were embarked for the passage up harbour and by 1000 the three carriers were secured alongside Melbourne Pier, with *Glory* ahead of *Implacable*.

The visit had received a great deal of advance publicity, and the people of Melbourne took the men of the Royal Navy to their hearts during the eight days that they spent alongside. Without doubt the highlight came during the afternoon and evening of Sunday 27 January, when the combined ships' companies marched through the city, followed by the Royal Marines Band Beating Retreat. The whole ceremony took place in front of the State Governor, Sir Winston Dugan, Vice-Admiral Vian and 10,000 spectators from Melbourne and the surrounding areas. The massed bands, with 72 musicians, were drawn from *Glory, Implacable, Indefatigable* and *Venerable*. The evening ceremony of Beating Retreat was broadcast throughout the country by the Australian Broadcasting Commission, but perhaps the most out-standing feature was the beautiful setting for the event. The Shrine of Remembrance stands on the Mound, overlooking the city, and away from it stretches a wide expanse of grass lawn flanked by miniature trees. On the gently sloping northern approach is the Pool of Reflection, and from it two massive flights of steps lead to the Shrine. It was at the top of the first flight, set in a chequered courtyard of grass squares, that the city's tallest flagstaff had been set up. Flying proudly from it, and visible to all of Melbourne, was a huge White Ensign, guarded at its base by four Royal Marines.

After marching on parade to "On the Quarterdeck" and "Vimy Ridge", the buglers sounded the Ceremonial Fanfare, which was followed by the slow and quick troops. The drummers beat the tattoo and the ceremonial guards marched through the bands to Alford's "Thin Red Line". After playing "Heart of Oak" at the halt, the bands played the evening hymn, "The Day Thou Gavest Lord is Ended", and as the setting sun dropped below a cloudless horizon, the guard fired a volley. This was followed by the "Sunset Call" and the National Anthem, before the parade marched off. That night Admiral Vian received the following message from the Governor of Victoria: "I would be glad if you will convey an expression of my warm appreciation and admiration to the Guard and Massed Bands of the Royal Marines of the 1st Aircraft Carrier

During the afternoon of Sunday 27 January 1946, led by mounted policemen, the combined ships' companies marched through Melbourne's city centre, where the crowds had turned out in force for the event.

A Corsair is launched by catapult.

Squadron who Beat Retreat at the Shrine at sunset this evening. I was much impressed by the drill and steadiness under arms of all ranks who took part in the parade as well as by the excellent and appropriate musical programme." From an ex-Grenadier Guardsman, this was praise indeed!

The visit came to an end during the forenoon of Thursday 31 January, and its success can be judged by the report which appeared in the Melbourne Argus, which referred not only to the, "...great service they did to enhance the reputation of the Royal Navy and Royal Marines, but also that of England and the British Empire. The visit will live long in the memories and true British hearts of the people of Melbourne and Australia."

After leaving Melbourne Admiral Vian transferred his flag to *Implacable*, before *Indefatigable* set course for Fremantle, Cape Town and home. For *Glory*,

"Jumbo" lifts a Corsair with a damaged undercarriage.

In March 1946 *Glory* was ordered to Auckland where she embarked No 14 Squadron, Royal New Zealand Air Force, their transport and stores, for the passage to Kure, Japan, where they were to form part of the Commonwealth Occupation Force.

During the passage Divisions were held on the flight deck and, in addition to the ship's company, the RNZAF personnel took part.

Implacable and their escorts there was the return passage to Jervis Bay for joint flying exercises, during which they were joined by the battleship *Anson* and the cruiser *Bermuda*. Both carriers remained in the Jervis Bay area for most of February, with *Glory's* Corsairs and Fireflies cross-operating with *Implacable's* Avengers. During Monday 11 February, Admiral Vian flew to *Glory* to watch the day's flying, then on 15 February, came the start of a four-day break in Sydney. During this time alongside all the squadron personnel were landed as *Glory* was about to become a troop transport once again. When she left Sydney during the afternoon of 25 February she flew off her aircraft before setting course across the Tasman Sea for Auckland, New Zealand. After the hectic flying programme of early February off the coast of New South Wales, the passage to Auckland was quiet and after seven days at sea she arrived at her destination. This time Captain Buzzard had been ordered to embark a contingent of No 14 Squadron, Royal New Zealand Air Force, together with some transport and stores, and deliver them to Kure at the south end of Japan's main island of Honshu. There they were to form part of the Commonwealth Occupation Force in Japan. The new passengers were very smart and eager when they embarked in the carrier on 5 and 7 March 1946, and when *Glory* sailed at 0940 on 8 March they were loudly cheered by those who had travelled to the docks to see them off. However, the 15-day passage saw the carrier steaming into some very severe weather, which kept many of them confined to their mess decks - and reduced the food consumption on board. When the weather eased they were eager participants in deck hockey tournaments which were organized on the flight deck. Although they were worthy opponents for departmental teams, following some of the more robust matches a few of them were seen to be limping badly. On the morning of Saturday 23 March *Glory* steamed into Japan's Inland Sea to make a daylight crossing of the picturesque waterway, and that evening she secured to No 4 buoy in Kure Harbour, close to the battleship *Duke of York*.

For most of *Glory's* officers and men the visit to Kure was their first sight of Japan, and it was very different from the neat and tidy pre-war days. One member of the ship's company recalls his memories of the city: "The Japanese fleet showed no signs of life as we

Glory enters Kure harbour during the afternoon of Saturday 23 March.

entered harbour, owing to the fact that it was lying on its side on the beaches after repeated visits of the US Air Force. Life on shore seemed to be just an existence, with labour gangs clearing away the rubble of what was once a first class naval base. There were curios for sale in the shops, but food was clearly more important to people than money and it was surprising how many nutty bars one could exchange for Japanese yen. Most of us went to the small naval canteen on the jetty, which became very popular with the ship's company." Some of the more adventurous members of the ship's company took the opportunity to join organized trips to the shattered city of Hiroshima, some 15 miles north of Kure. For those who made the trip, it was a sobering sight and one which they would never forget.

Glory left Kure during the morning of Friday 29 March, and after pausing off Iwakuni to embark an absentee, she set course for Sydney. As she steamed south past the island of Tarega-Shima additional lookouts were posted as a number of floating horned mines were sighted, obviously having broken adrift from their moorings. Fortunately, with calm seas and clear weather they were easily seen and avoided. During the passage south there was a full Crossing the Line ceremony, complete with Neptune, Queen Aphrodite and the Bears who took great pains to hunt down the important and the uninitiated. This was combined with an inter-departmental sports day at which the Royal Marines excelled at the egg & spoon, sack and three-legged races. Finally, on Friday 12 April, after an absence of over six weeks, *Glory* arrived back in Sydney Harbour - it was almost becoming her home port.

As always when she returned to Sydney there were members of the ship's company due for demobilisation, who left the ship to await a passage home and on this occasion, with *Glory* about to start an eight-week maintenance period, there was a large turnover of personnel. On 17 April, when she was moved to the Garden Island Naval Base, to the delight of the ship's company, both watches were granted ten days station leave, which was always very popular in Sydney. At 1100 on 5 May, the lower deck was cleared and the ship's company cheered, and watched with some envy, as *Implacable* and *Duke of York* left harbour for their voyage home via Trincomalee and Suez. Twelve days later *Glory* was towed into the Captain Cook dry dock for maintenance, and the ship's company took part in the Sydney Victory Parade.

On completion of the maintenance period *Glory* left Sydney, with the cruiser *Euryalus*, on Friday 14 June, and within hours all the aircraft had been safely landed on. The two ships then set course for the town of

During her southward passage back to Sydney in April 1946 a full Crossing the Line ceremony was held.

After a refit in Sydney, *Glory* left on Saturday 22 June 1946 for Trincomalee via Adelaide. As well as the Corsairs of 1831 Squadron and the Fireflies of 837 Squadron, a Walrus seaplane is ranged on deck by the ensign.

Corsairs prepare for a dawn launch.

Newcastle, some 125 miles north of Sydney, where they secured alongside Lee Jetty. The visit coincided with the England Rugby Team's tour of the area, and so the ships' companies were able to turn out in force to support their national team - and the Royal Marines Band gave a splendid performance during the interval. However, it was all in vain as the England side lost to the home team! After 48 hours in Newcastle, on Monday 17 June *Glory* and *Euryalus* were at sea once again and flying operations were under way. For three days the two vessels exercised off the coast of New South Wales, but on the final day there was a tragic accident when one of *Glory's* aircraft handlers, Able Seaman Sherley, was killed when he was hit by the rotating propeller blades of an aircraft. Next morning, at 0835 on Thursday 20 June, in a position just off Sydney Heads, the burial service was held for the unfortunate rating. Just over an hour later *Glory* secured alongside a berth at Woolloomooloo Docks

for a short break.

After only 48 hours alongside in Sydney *Glory*, together with the destroyer *Finisterre*, sailed once again from the city that many members of the ship's company considered to be their home port, to make a well-publicized visit to Adelaide in South Australia. After anchoring off the port the previous night, the two ships steamed up harbour during the forenoon of 27 June to secure alongside the main jetty of the outer harbour. During the seven-day visit the ship was opened to the public, and attracted huge queues of people eager to look round the carrier. Ashore, to the delight of the residents of Adelaide, the ship's company marched through the city. However, when they left the port on 3 July they also left Australian waters, setting course for Trincomalee and the East Indies Fleet.

During the passage flying exercises were undertaken but at 1020 on Thursday 11 July, a Firefly of 837 Squadron got into difficulties some miles away from

On Sunday 30 June 1946, during her seven-day stay in Adelaide, the ship was opened to visitors. Here long queues patiently wait for their turn to look round the ship.

the ship. Fortunately the pilot was able to bail out and was picked up by *Finisterre*. That afternoon, despite having fractured a leg, he was transferred to *Glory* by jackstay.

Five days later, having flown off all serviceable aircraft, *Glory* secured to No 1 buoy in Trincomalee Harbour. For the ship's company it was to be a very different run ashore from what they had become used to in Australia. As one member recalls: "After experiencing the bright lights of Australia

Framed by coconut palms *Glory* lies at anchor in the picturesque setting of Trincomalee harbour.

for so long, being dumped in that place was like having a dark blanket thrown upon us. Nevertheless, we made the best of it, as there was plenty of opportunity for sports and just wandering round the island."

On Monday 29 July 1946, Rear-Admiral A. R. M. Bridge, Flag Officer (Air) of the joint British Pacific and East Indies Fleets, joined the ship with his staff. Next day the carrier and her escort *Finisterre* sailed from the anchorage for three days of flying practice in the exercise areas off Ceylon (Sri Lanka). This routine continued during the first three weeks of August, with short breaks at Trincomalee. During one of these breaks an RAF Concert Party performed their show, "Not so Much the Heat", in the hangar. Wednesday 21 August saw the start of a six-day break in Colombo, where there was a much more exciting run ashore. Some members of the ship's company visited the places that are generally frequented by sailors, while others went to the beaches of Mount Lavinia or took sightseeing tours deep inland to the famous temples of Kandy.

When *Glory* and *Finisterre* left Colombo it was back to the familiar programmes of flying training off the coast of Ceylon. At 0900 on Saturday 7 September 1946, during a break at Trincomalee, there was a change of command when Captain W. D. Couchman DSO OBE RN, who had joined the ship the previous

afternoon, relieved Captain Buzzard. Later that day, at 1700, Captain Buzzard left the ship to await a passage home and promotion to Rear-Admiral. On 21 September *Glory* and her faithful escort, *Finisterre*, rendezvoused with *Venerable* and the destroyer *Lagos* and all four vessels set course for Hong Kong. During the passage both carriers cross-operated their aircraft, but on 26 September *Venerable* stopped off at Singapore Naval Base - whilst *Glory* continued on her way to Hong Kong. On Friday 27 September there was another fatal accident on the flight deck, when Air Mechanic J. F. Adams was killed by the rotating airscrew of a Firefly aircraft. Later that day, at 1710, with the ship in a position Lat 06º-12'N/Long 107º-45'E, his burial service was held on the quarterdeck. Eventually, during the forenoon of Tuesday 1 October, *Glory* secured to No 2 buoy in Hong Kong Harbour. Next day *Venerable* arrived and moored close by.

During the first three weeks of October, both *Glory* and *Venerable*, escorted by the destroyers *Comet* and *Contest*, carried out flying exercises off Hong Kong. On completion of each day's flying programme they would anchor in Junk Bay for the night, and at weekends they would return to their respective buoys in the harbour. On Thursday 17 October, *Venerable* left Hong Kong for Singapore where she was to undertake

806 Naval Air Squadron pose for an official photograph.

At anchor and dressed overall at Trincomalee.

Looking aft along *Glory's* flight deck with Fireflies ranged as she exercises with her sister *Venerable* and the destroyers *Finisterre* and *Lagos* during the passage from Trincomalee to Hong Kong.

a short refit, before returning to the colony in the last week of November. On Sunday 20 October the C-in-C British Pacific Fleet, Vice-Admiral Sir Denis Boyd, inspected the ship's company at Divisions on the flight deck. During the following week *Glory* put to sea for the ship's Sea Otter to carry out landing practice and, with the ship at anchor in Junk Bay, it landed on the flight deck and in the sheltered waters of the bay. That week the carrier returned to harbour during the afternoon of Wednesday 23 October to prepare for a ceremonial Beating Retreat by the massed bands of the Royal Marines from *Glory* and the cruisers *Belfast* and *Bermuda*. The event took place during the evening of 25 October on *Glory's* flight deck and, as well as Vice-Admiral Boyd, it was attended by the Governor of Hong Kong, Sir Mark Young, and the commanding officers of the Army and RAF units stationed in the colony. During that week the disarmed Japanese aircraft carrier *Katsuragi*, which was being used for repatriation duties, entered harbour to embark some of the last Japanese prisoners of war left in Hong Kong. Once these duties were completed *Katsuragi* would be broken up.

For the last few days of October and the first two weeks of November *Glory* operated out of Hong Kong, accompanied by the destroyers *Constance* and *Contest*, and on occasions by the cruiser *Belfast* (flag Vice-Admiral Sir Denis Boyd). On Wednesday 13 November, accompanied by the destroyer *Lagos*, the carrier left Hong Kong to set course for Singapore where, five days later, she entered King George VI dry dock, which had recently been vacated by *Venerable*. The run ashore in Singapore meant a pleasant change of scenery for the ship's company, and the dockyard canteen did a roaring trade in ice-cold Tiger beer during the three-week refit.

It was Monday 9 December when *Glory* left Singapore Naval Base to recover her aircraft and to carry out exercises with RAF aircraft from their base at Tengah. That afternoon a Corsair was forced to ditch in a bay on the east coast of Malaya, but fortunately the pilot escaped with minor injuries. Four days later *Glory* was heading for Hong Kong and after a four-day passage and a night at anchor off Junk Island, she rendezvoused with *Venerable* again. The two carriers then operated in local waters for 24 hours before they entered Hong Kong and secured at buoys in the harbour for the Christmas and New Year cele-

During the forenoon of Sunday 20 October 1946, the C-in-C British Pacific Fleet, Vice-Admiral Sir Denis Boyd, inspected the ship's company at Divisions.

On the evening of Friday 25 October 1946, the massed bands of the Royal Marines from *Glory*, *Belfast* and *Bermuda* Beat Retreat on *Glory's* flight deck. The principal guests were the Governor, Sir Mark Young, and Admiral Boyd.

brations. *Glory's* ship's company spent Christmas Day at one hour's notice for steam after a number of typhoon warnings were received, but by New Year's Eve this had been extended to four hours and all but the duty watch were able to join in the festivities ashore.

It was at 0815 on Thursday 2 January 1947 that *Glory* and *Venerable*, escorted by *Alert*, *Finisterre* and

Widemouth Bay, left Hong Kong to carry out flying exercises off the coast. It was during the afternoon of the seventh day of the manoeuvres that a Corsair from *Glory* ditched in the sea, about 13 miles from the ship. Fortunately, the injured pilot was rescued by *Finisterre* and taken directly to Hong Kong. Later that day both carriers returned to harbour for a 19-day maintenance period. On board *Glory* the men had an

Two Seafires from *Glory's* 806 Naval Air Squadron flying over one of Hong Kong's many outlying islands.

A landing exercise on one of Hong Kong's outlying islands.

extra workload as the ship was prepared for inspection by Rear-Admiral Bridge on 21 January. After having been delayed for two days by bad weather, both *Glory* and *Venerable* sailed from Hong Kong on 28 January to continue their joint flying exercises. These continued until well into February with weekends spent in harbour, but on 14 February *Venerable* set course for Trincomalee and home, where she was transferred to the Royal Netherlands Navy.

After *Venerable's* departure *Glory* remained in Hong Kong for four days, before she and her escort *Finisterre* followed her course through the South China Sea, bound for Trincomalee. En route there were exercises with RAF Beaufighters and Sunderland flying boats from Seletar in Singapore. The two ships arrived in Trincomalee on 27 February, where Rear-Admiral Bridge transferred his flag to *Venerable,* which then promptly left for Devonport. *Glory* undertook further flying off the island of Ceylon, where she exercised with *Contest* and the cruiser *Jamaica,* before setting course north for Bombay. During the passage another tragedy struck during the afternoon of 7 March, when Firefly 272 crashed during flying practice, killing the pilot, Lt-Cdr Bates, and the observer, Lt Mayne. Next day *Glory* anchored off Bombay Harbour, close to the celebrated Gateway of India.

The carrier had been sent to Bombay, not only to show the flag during the last weeks of Britain's Indian Empire, but to mark the arrival of the new, and last, Viceroy, Lord Mountbatten. This final change of viceroys in India represented a change from tradition. Normally, an outgoing viceroy sailed with due pomp from the Gateway of India, while the incoming P&O steamer bore his successor towards its massive arches. This spared India the embarrassment of having two "Gods" upon its soil at the same time. On this occasion, however, not only had Lord Mountbatten flown from Northolt direct to New Delhi, but he had insisted on meeting the outgoing Viceroy, Field Marshal Sir Archibald Wavell. As far as *Glory* was concerned the changeover day, 20 March, began at 0810 when 160 VIP guests embarked in the carrier. It was time to wiegh anchor and put to sea to give a flying demonstration, before the aircraft rendezvoused with RAF planes to stage a fly-past over the port and city of Bombay. Next day, with the viceregal duties completed, *Glory*, *Jamaica* and *Contest* left Bombay to make the passage south back to the naval base on Ceylon's north-east coast.

After arriving at Trincomalee on Tuesday 25 March, *Glory* met her younger sister *Theseus* for the first time, and Rear-Admiral Creasy, the Flag Officer (Air) for the newly designated Far East Station, having travelled out from the UK in *Theseus*, transferred his flag to *Glory*. Also during *Glory's* stay at Trincomalee the Corsairs of 1831 Squadron were exchanged for the Seafire FX Vs of 806 Squadron, with the squadron personnel joining the ship during the afternoon of 1 April. Next day *Glory* left her berth in Trincomalee Harbour to begin a busy programme of flying training, which would continue each week, with weekends

A range of Seafires of 806 Squadron and Fireflies of 837 Squadron starting up prior to take-off.

Folding the wings of a Firefly before striking the aircraft down into the hangar.

A Firefly being struck down into the hangar.

The flight deck personnel extricate a Firefly from the crash barrier.

"Lined-up-left". A Firefly has taken a wire, but the port oleo has fallen into the catwalk. The propeller blades have broken on the deck edge and firefighters run towards the aircraft in case ruptured fuel lines ignite.

Another Firefly barrier prang. Not every landing was this bad...

Lieutenant Commander Hain, the Commanding Officer of 837 Squadron, with some of his aircrew.

being spent at anchor in the harbour. On 22 April she took part in manoeuvres with *Theseus* and the cruisers *Glasgow* and *Jamaica* and the destroyer *Contest*. Next day, whilst launching a range of eight Seafires for a mock raid on Fort Frederick, a member of the flight deck personnel, Able Seaman Taylor, was struck by the wing of a Seafire and killed. Later that afternoon, shortly before the ship anchored off Trincomalee, the burial service was held.

On Tuesday 29 April, Seafire SW 821 piloted by Lt Cdr (A) Thurston, crashed on deck whilst landing on and went over the port side of the ship into the sea. The main engines were immediately stopped and the seaboat was lowered, but unfortunately there was no sign of either the pilot or the aircraft. Next day saw the final day's flying before *Glory* was prepared for a maintenance period. During the first two days of May, with the carrier secured to a buoy at Trincomalee, all the aircraft were disembarked into barges and taken ashore. Admiral Creasy and his staff transferred to *Theseus*. Finally, on 12 May, *Glory* weighed anchor and set course for Singapore Naval Base where she arrived five days later. Two days after going alongside No 13 berth, the ship was towed into King George VI dry dock and the ship's company moved into the

shore accommodation at *HMS Terror*.

Glory remained in the dry dock for 31 days, during which time a large number of her officers and men left the ship for passages home, and their places were taken by personnel fresh out from the UK. It was Thursday 19 June before *Glory* was ready for sea again and she sailed that morning to embark the Seafires of 806 Squadron and the Fireflies of 837 Squadron, before carrying out a mini work-up over three days off Singapore. Four days later, having weighed anchor at 0615, she rendezvoused with *Theseus* and the destroyers *Cockade* and *Contest*, before all four vessels set course for Australia. With large numbers of the ship's company having recently joined the ship a Crossing the Line ceremony was held on the flight deck on 24 June as she steamed south. Once off the Australian coast *Theseus* and *Cockade* parted company and set course for Tasmania and a visit to Hobart. *Glory* and *Contest*, meanwhile, headed for Adelaide, arriving off the port on 4 July. At 0715 that morning, as the two ships steamed towards the harbour, 11 Fireflies and nine Seafires were launched to make an early fly-past over Adelaide to wake up the city. Once alongside there was a substantial programme of entertainment for the ship's company, which included sightseeing tours, dances, visits to the races, many private parties and a full sports programme. *Glory* proved to be very popular with the residents of Adelaide. During the weekend of 5 and 6 July, when the ship was opened to visitors, long queues formed along the jetty.

When the visit ended on 9 July, 60 VIP guests boarded the carrier to be taken to sea for a forenoon flying display, after which they were disembarked and *Glory* and her escort left the area to rendezvous with *Theseus* and *Cockade* off Melbourne. Following their meeting the two carriers and their escorts steamed into Melbourne's Outer Harbour where, at 1000 on Friday 11 July, they secured alongside the Station Pier. The nine-day visit to the state capital of Victoria was broken briefly for nine hours on 15 July when the two carriers put to sea in order to rehearse for a mass fly-past over the city. Three days later detachments from all four units, together with the Royal Marines Bands, marched through the city, where Admiral Creasy and the State Governor took the salute. That same afternoon, there was a "first" in *Glory's* chapel when Lt (E) I. C. Dalzell married Miss Helen Houston, with the service being taken by the ship's chaplain, Reverend Birch. There was little time for a honeymoon, however, for two days later, at 1000 on Sunday 20 July, the two carriers and their escorts left Melbourne, bound for Sydney. That afternoon, as they steamed out to sea,

all the aircraft from both *Glory* and *Theseus* were launched to perform the fly-past over Melbourne. Sadly tragedy marred the occasion when two Fireflies from *Theseus* collided in mid-air killing all four crew members, three officers and a senior rating. Just over half an hour later, on board *Theseus*, a rating was killed when a Firefly crashed on landing. Meanwhile, on board *Glory*, aircraft were giving a flying demonstration to a group of RAAF officers who were taking passage to Sydney. At 1450, as the Seafires were landing on, one aircraft crashed on deck seriously injuring two ratings of the flight deck personnel. One of the men, Naval Airman T. Saddler, was gravely injured and he was quickly transferred to *Contest* which steamed at full speed for Melbourne where he was transferred to hospital. Unfortunately, later that evening it was learned that he had died from his injuries and a memorial service was held on the quarterdeck.

After exercising with aircraft of the RAAF off the coast of New South Wales, the two carriers entered Sydney Harbour where, during the forenoon of Thursday 24 July, *Glory* and *Theseus* secured alongside Nos 1 and 2 berths at Woolloomooloo. The end of *Glory's* long deployment east of Suez was now in sight, and during the 12 days alongside large quantities of stores under the "Food for Britain" scheme were embarked. There were also two very well attend-

A ship's boxing tournament on the flight deck.

A jackstay transfer with a destroyer steaming very slowly alongside.

ed ship's company dances held in the hangar, and both carriers were opened to the public.

Finally, during the afternoon of 5 August, both *Glory* and *Theseus*, together with the two destroyers, left Sydney for Brisbane, where they spent ten days. After leaving the coast of Queensland, at 1540 on 18 August, *Theseus* and *Cockade* parted company as they set course for New Zealand and *Glory* and *Contest* headed for Singapore. It was the first stage of the carrier's voyage home.

At Singapore over 100 passengers, consisting of Naval, Army and RAF personnel, were embarked, together with the colours of the 1st Battalion, King's Royal Regiment, for passage to Devonport. After leaving the naval base on 2 September, *Glory* called at Trincomalee and Aden, arriving in Suez Bay during the early hours of 22 September. She started her Suez Canal transit that forenoon, and by the afternoon of 23 September she had left Port Said and was heading for

Malta. She arrived in Grand Harbour three days later, and during her three-day stay she met her younger sister *Ocean* for the first time. After leaving Malta there was only a short five-hour stopover in Gibraltar Bay before she anchored in Plymouth Sound on 6 October 1947, after an absence from the UK of two and a half years. The commission was not over, however, for after clearing customs and disembarking her passengers, she left the Sound and set course north through the Irish Sea, arriving alongside Glasgow's King George V Dock at 1845 on 8 October. During her two days alongside all the aircraft were offloaded on to the quayside, and the "Food for Britain" was disembarked. At 0820 on 10 October, after the squadron personnel had left the ship, *Glory* left Glasgow to anchor off Greenock overnight, before setting course for Devonport.

After a slow voyage south, and three hours at anchor in Plymouth Sound, *Glory* steamed up harbour during the forenoon of 13 October, and at midday she was manoeuvred into the North Lock dry dock. During the weeks that followed the ship's company was steadily reduced, and on 15 January 1948, Captain Couchman relinquished his command and handed over to Commander G. F. Blaxland RN.

The Governor of Singapore, Sir Franklin Gimson, takes the salute as *Glory's* Guard of Honour march past City Hall for the King's 1946 Birthday Parade.

Mediterranean Fleet
January 1948 - December 1950

Following a period of maintenance in dry dock, in early 1948 *Glory* was towed into No 5 basin where, under a small care and maintenance party, she remained until the early summer of 1949. For a time during 1948 she was used as an accommodation ship for the ship's company of *HMAS Sydney*, the Majestic-class light fleet carrier which had been built by Devonport Dockyard as *HMS Terrible*. With the commissioning of *Sydney* in December 1948 *Glory* was once again left without a role. In the early summer of 1949 she was brought out of reserve and refitted for further operational service. During the refit her bridge was rebuilt and her pom-pom anti-air-craft guns were replaced with 16 single 40mm Bofors guns.

At 1650 on Monday 15 August 1949, her new commanding officer, Captain E. H. Shattock OBE RN, joined the ship. By the end of August 1949 *Glory* was once again alongside the sea wall in Devonport Dockyard, firmly secured to 6 & 7 wharves. On Friday 2 September she was struck by the elderly cruiser *Leander* which, prior to decommissioning, was under tow and on her way into No 5 basin. Fortunately, apart from some dents and minor abrasions to her paintwork, the carrier was not seriously damaged. Six weeks later Rear-Admiral (E) D. C.

Glory arrived in Malta's Grand Harbour on 11 November 1949 to join the Mediterranean Fleet. Here she lies secured to No 8 buoy, opposite Valletta's Customs House Steps.

Maxwell arrived on board to inspect all the main machinery spaces, and four days after that, at 1000 on Monday 17 October 1949, *Glory* was recommissioned in the presence of the C-in-C Plymouth, who inspected Divisions on the flight deck.

On Wednesday 19 October, *Glory* left Devonport for her post-refit trials. During the first two days the carrier underwent full-power trials in the Channel and when completed, anchored in St Austell Bay to await the arrival of her official trials party. During the following evening a distress message was received from a small coaster, *SS Yew Park*, which was in difficulties off Land's End. The boiler room personnel immediately started to raise steam, but before this could be completed other vessels had gone to the aid of the merchantman and *Glory* was stood down. On Wednesday 26 October she resumed her sea trials and next day the first landing on the flight deck for two and a half years was made by an Avenger. Half an hour later the aircraft was launched from the catapult, and at 1050 there was an even more dramatic landing on board when a Vampire jet touched down safely. For the remainder of the day the Avenger continued to carry out landing trials on board, and the Vampire was successfully launched. *Glory* then anchored in Sandown Bay off the Isle of Wight. Next day saw the carrier undergoing another ten hours of flying trials, before she made a ceremonial entry into Portsmouth Harbour to spend a weekend alongside South Railway Jetty.

Whilst she was in Portsmouth 150 ratings joined *Glory* and the Duke of Edinburgh's yacht *Coweslip* was loaded aboard for passage to Malta. At 1347 on Monday 31 October she sailed for Glasgow. After negotiating her passage of the River Clyde the carrier secured alongside Govan's King George V Dock on 2 November, and for the following 24 hours the stores, equipment and some aircraft for the 14th Carrier Air Group were embarked. The Air Group itself comprised the Sea Fury FB11s of 804 Squadron and Mk 6 Fireflies of 812 Squadron, which were in Hal Far, Malta, having been left there by *Ocean* the previous month. *Glory* left Glasgow during the forenoon of Thursday 3 November, and after carrying out several runs over the Arran measured mile, set course for the Mediterranean. After an eight-day uninterrupted voyage the carrier anchored in Marsaxlokk Bay on the morning of 11 November. Next day she entered Grand

On Wednesday 14 December 1949, HRH Princess Elizabeth inspected *Glory's* ship's company at ceremonial Divisions on the flight deck.

Harbour where she took *Triumph's* place in the Mediterranean Fleet, the latter having sailed for the Far East.

On 15 November *Glory's* work started in earnest and she was at sea with Sea Furies and Fireflies of 804 and 812 Squadrons beginning what would prove to be two very busy weeks of intensive flying. On 29 November, having flown the aircraft off to Hal Far, *Glory* entered the *Admiralty Floating Dock No 35* in Grand Harbour. This massive dry dock had been towed in two sections from Bombay in early 1947, before India's independence, and it had to be reconstructed in the dockyard. *Glory* was the first major ship to use the floating dock following its recommissioning on 4 October 1949. The underwater maintenance necessary kept her high and dry until 7 December. Once out of dry dock *Glory* was shifted to Parlatorio Wharf and then to No 8 buoy in Grand Harbour, close to Customs House Steps, which would

Looking aft from the island superstructure as *Glory* makes a ceremonial departure from Grand Harbour.

Using Rocket Assisted Take-Off Gear (RATOG), a Firefly takes off from bow to stern as *Glory* lies moored in Grand Harbour.

Glory leaves Malta during her Mediterranean deployment.

become very familiar territory to her liberty men. It was whilst she was moored at the buoy, on Wednesday 14 December, that *Glory* received a royal visitor, HRH Princess Elizabeth, who at that time was a serving officer's wife as the Duke of Edinburgh was commanding *Magpie* based at Malta. The ship was dressed overall and detachments from other units in harbour were present on board to represent their various ships. At 1130 *Glory's* saluting guns crashed out a 21-gun royal salute and three minutes later Princess Elizabeth arrived on board, where she was met by the C-in-C, Admiral Sir Arthur Power, and Captain Shattock. After inspecting the ceremonial Divisions on the flight deck, the Princess reviewed other units of the Mediterranean Fleet, before leaving the carrier. Next day, however, came the most popular part of the proceedings when, at noon, the main brace was spliced.

Five days after the royal visit *Glory* was at sea once again, while her squadrons engaged in busy flying programmes. During the afternoon of Friday 23 December she returned to her buoy in Grand Harbour and the ship's company had a five-day break over Christmas. On Tuesday 27 December, Captain

Shattock fell ill and he was taken ashore to RNH Bighi. In his place Captain H. Traill CBE RN, was appointed to command the carrier temporarily. He was waiting to take command of the maintenance carrier *Perseus*, which was at Belfast being fitted with a prototype steam catapult, before undergoing secret trials with this new equipment. No sooner had Captain Traill settled in than *Glory* was at sea again for a full three-day flying programme, which ended on 30 December when she went back to her buoy in Grand Harbour for the New Year celebrations.

Glory's break was soon over, and on Wednesday 4 January 1950 she slipped her moorings and left harbour to carry out a full day's flying programme south of Malta. Acting as planeguard that day was the Indian Navy's destroyer *Ranjit* (formerly *HMS Redoubt*), which had just been acquired by India and which was on her way to Bombay. That afternoon, with the carrier some 8 miles off Delmira Point, Firefly 204 crashed into the sea over *Glory's* starboard side. Within two minutes *Ranjit* was at the scene of the accident, but her sea boat's crew were only able to recover the body of the pilot, Lt G. W. Turney. Of the observer, Lt T. O.

Glory off Gibraltar. Note the Levanter cloud over the Rock.

Heavy weather in the Mediterranean.

Brigstock, there was no trace, nor could any wreckage be found. Just over half an hour later *Glory* anchored in Marsaxlokk Bay for the night and a memorial service was held on the quarterdeck. Next day, after a full flying schedule, the carrier returned to Grand Harbour, where she secured to No 11 buoy in Bighi Bay. On Saturday 7 January the colours were lowered to half mast for the funeral of Lt Turney.

During her period at Malta the Flag Officer (Air) Mediterranean, Rear-Admiral G. Grantham, hoisted his flag on board the carrier which would remain his flagship until she left the Mediterranean. On 10 January *Glory* sailed again to carry out three more days of intensive flying exercises, and this was followed by a ten-day maintenance period in Grand Harbour. When she left Malta on 23 January *Glory* set course north to make her first foreign visit of the commission. Two days later, after an extremely rough passage, she arrived at Naples. During her five days in the Italian port there was plenty of ceremonial activi-

A Firefly is launched from the catapult. The strop which connects the aircraft to the shuttle can be seen falling away as the aircraft gets airborne.

In ideal weather conditions a Firefly lands on. Both barriers have been raised to protect the deck park.

ty and on one day the Royal Marines provided nine guards and bands in the space of just three hours. Most of the ship's company enjoyed the stay, and when *Glory* left the port on 30 January there were many who felt it should have lasted longer. On the last day of January, as she steamed towards the Libyan port of Tripoli, she took part in joint flying exercises with the *USS Midway* which, like *Glory*, had been completed just too late to take an active part in the Second World War. Next day *Glory* anchored off Tripoli, but with the ship remaining in sea watches there was no shore leave. On 2 February, off the Libyan coast, the carrier undertook manoeuvres with the destroyers *Cheviot* and *Vigo*. Anchoring off Tripoli during the following morning shore leave was granted until midnight. After three more days off the Libyan port, *Glory* returned to Malta and during flying exercises on the forenoon of 8 February one of the carrier's Sea Furies ditched into the sea some miles away from the ship. Fortunately, the pilot baled out safely and after a long period in the sea he was picked up by *Cheviot*. The flying programme ended during the afternoon of 10 February, when *Glory* returned to Grand Harbour to secure to No 8 buoy.

During her extended weekend at Malta, on Sunday 12 February, Captain Shattock returned to duty and the following afternoon Captain Traill left the ship. On Tuesday 14 February *Glory* left harbour and

steamed to sea where the Air Group landed on, to carry out a three-day flying programme with ships of the Mediterranean Fleet. This was followed by a ten-day maintenance period in Grand Harbour, during which the ship was prepared for her spring cruise, which began on 27 February. After leaving Malta *Glory* rendezvoused with the destroyers *Chequers*, *Gravelines* and *Vigo*, the cruiser *Liverpool* and, from the Home Fleet, the fleet carrier *Implacable*, and *Vengeance*, her sister ship. After exercising off Malta the fleet put into Palmas Bay, Sardinia, the first stop on the cruise, and from there they steamed west to anchor off Golfe Juan on the Cote d'Azur, close to Cannes. Although it was an expensive run ashore the ship's company enjoyed the visit, and groups got as far afield as Nice and Monte Carlo. With sea temperatures rising, "Hands to Bathe" was piped each day, and the ship was opened to the public during one afternoon. After leaving the French Riviera during the evening of 13 March *Glory* took part in a night encounter exercise, and an air defence exercise in company with *Vengeance*, during which Sea Hornets from *Implacable* carried out mock attacks on the two smaller carriers.

The second port of call on the cruise was Algiers, when *Glory* anchored in the Old Port during the forenoon of 16 March for a four-day visit. After leaving Algiers there were further exercises, before the whole fleet put in to Gibraltar on 22 March. *Glory's* first cruise of the year ended on the last day of March, when, together with *Liverpool* and the destroyers, she entered Grand Harbour for a maintenance period which was to last until mid-May. On 31 March the ship's company received news of their future, when the Admiralty announced that in December 1950, after having been refitted in Malta, *Glory* would return to the UK and recommission with a Chatham ship's company. The signal went on to state that the ship would then return to the Mediterranean, but it was also possible that in May 1951 she would steam east of Suez to relieve *Theseus* on the Far East Station.

On 13 April the Prime Minister of Malta paid a visit to *Glory*, and on 24 April the ship was shifted to *AFD 35* again for maintenance on the hull. On 4 May there was a large ceremonial parade in Valletta's Palace Square where, in the presence of HRH Princess Elizabeth and the Duke of Edinburgh, the bands and drums of the Mediterranean Fleet carried out the ceremony of Beating Retreat. The massed bands and a royal guard of honour were provided by HM Ships *Glory*, *Liverpool*, *Gambia*, *Ceylon*, *Euryalus* and

Forth. Four days later *Glory* was moved out of dry dock and back to No 8 buoy in the harbour.

By Tuesday 16 May *Glory* was ready for sea again, and that forenoon she sailed from Grand Harbour to land on her aircraft. For the rest of that month she spent most weekdays at sea carrying out full flying programmes. On Wednesday 24 May, during one such exercise, when the carrier was some 9 miles south of Filfa Island, there was a tragic accident when Sea Fury 106, flown by Lieutenant Mudford, crashed over the port side of the ship when attempting to land on. Although the ship was quickly stopped and the crash boat was away within minutes, there was no trace of the pilot. Later that day another memorial service was held on the quarterdeck, before the carrier anchored in Marsaxlokk Bay for the night. The flying exercises and fleet manoeuvres continued for three weeks, but on Monday 12 June, *Glory*, together with other units of the Mediterranean Fleet, including the cruiser *Gambia* (flag C-in-C Mediterranean, Admiral Sir John Edelsten) and destroyers from the 3rd Destroyer Flotilla, including *Armada*, *Chevron*, *Chivalrous*, *Gravelines*, *Saintes* and *Vigo*, left Malta for Corfu.

For five days, between 8 and 13 September, *Glory* visited the French naval base at Marseilles.

Between 9 October and 23 November 1950, in order that maintenance work could be carried out on her underwater hull, *Glory* was high and dry in Admiralty Floating Dock No 35 in Grand Harbour.

They were to take part in exercises with the Royal Hellenic Navy, which would include four Greek destroyers and three submarines. The British squadron entered Corfu harbour on 14 June for a five-day break before the exercises began. On 19 June, on sailing from Corfu, *Glory* formed part of "Green Force", with the British and Greek destroyers, and steamed south where they were to be intercepted by the four submarines of "Blue Force". At 1835 on the first day of the exercise the last aircraft in a serial of Fireflies crashed through the barrier when landing on and before it came to a halt the plane hit a number of aircraft in the forward deck park, seriously injuring three ratings. In view of the men's injuries it was decided to detach *Glory* from the exercise and, with *Chivalrous*, she returned to Malta to land the casualties. Next day, at 1145, *Glory* secured to a buoy in Grand Harbour for the three men to be transferred to RNH Bighi. Four hours later the carrier steamed round to Marsaxlokk bay where the damaged aircraft were disembarked into lighters and taken ashore.

It was Wednesday 21 June before *Glory* and *Chivalrous* were able to rejoin the exercise and two days later, with the first phase completed, the joint fleet anchored off Skiathos Island in the Aegean Sea. During the six days at anchor, on Sunday 25 June, the Korean War broke out, but off Skiathos it was not thought that *Glory* would be affected by what seemed, at first, to be a localized conflict. There was more concern about the strong winds and rain squalls which were disrupting the general drill and sailing regattas. Before the second phase of the exercises began *Glory* made the 36-hour passage to Piraeus for a five-day visit before moving to the Turkish port of Marmaris, where the postponed sailing regattas took place. From there she steamed to Larnaca in Cyprus, where she anchored in the bay. On 18 July, after leaving Larnaca, *Glory* rejoined the fleet and phase two of the Anglo-Greek naval exercises began with the ships operating from Khrysokhou Bay. The manoeuvres ended during the evening of 20 July, when she set course for Egypt and next morning she moored in Alexandria Harbour.

Flying her paying-off pennant, on Tuesday 12 December 1950, *Glory* left Gibraltar for her return passage to Devonport. She was steaming into severe gales and extremely heavy seas.

It was her first visit since July 1945 and, as it was one of her last "foreign" visits of the commission, it was not long before leather goods of all shapes and sizes, together with a large number of red fezzes, made an appearance on the mess decks. After five days in port *Glory* left harbour and set course for Malta. On the last day of July the aircraft were flown off to Hal Far, and at 1130 the carrier was secured to buoys in Grand Harbour.

During August only seven days were spent at sea, with flying exercises being carried out in local waters. In early September there was a short cruise which took the ship to Marseilles, Tangier and Gibraltar. These were very brief calls, however, and by 26 September the carrier was at sea carrying out a programme of flying in the Western Mediterranean. On the afternoon of Wednesday 27 September a Sea Fury from 804 Squadron was lost at sea, and despite a lengthy and extensive search by *Glory* and the destroyer *Saintes*, there was no trace of the pilot. By the end of September *Glory* was back in Maltese waters, and on 1 October she berthed in Grand Harbour to begin a two-month refit. For eight days the carrier remained secured to No 7 buoy whilst destoring and deammunitioning took place, then on 9 October she was moved to *AFD 35* for dry docking. For six weeks the ship resounded to a cacophony of noise as windy hammers, chisels and scrapers beat a

tattoo on the ship's hull, and even the establishments in "The Gut" became havens of peace on Saturday evenings. Some lucky members of the ship's company were able to take some station leave, but most had to live on board and put up with the noise. On 23 November, with the underwater hull and the ship's sides having been repainted, *Glory* was shifted to Parlatorio Wharf for the refit to be completed.

Glory's refit lasted for nine weeks, but on Friday 8 December, in company with the destroyer *Saintes*, she left Grand Harbour to embark the squadrons and to set course for Gibraltar. That afternoon Admiral Grantham hauled down his flag and transferred to *Saintes* by jackstay. Three days later the carrier secured alongside Gibraltar's south mole. Twenty-four hours later she was at sea again and heading for Devonport, but it was a rough passage as Force 11 winds and enormous seas battered the immaculate paintwork of her hull. In the Bay of Biscay all the carley floats were washed away by the huge waves, but relief came during the evening of 15 December when the carrier anchored in Plymouth Sound. Next day, after Customs officers had done their worst, *Glory* weighed anchor and steamed up harbour where she secured alongside 5 & 6 wharves of Devonport Dockyard. The Mediterranean commission was over.....

Chapter Six

War in Korea
December 1950 - October 1951

Within a week of her arrival at Devonport *Glory* had paid off and on Thursday 28 December 1950 her new commanding officer, Captain K. S. Colquhoun DSO RN, joined. That same afternoon Captain Shattock left to take up a new appointment at the War College. Two days after the change of command a draft of 250 ratings joined the ship, the first contingent of the Chatham ship's company, and by the second week of January 1951 the complement was up to strength. Finally, on Thursday 25 January, a cold and misty winter's day, *Glory* was ready for sea and left Devonport to carry out a full-power trial and to embark her Sea Otter. She then anchored in Weymouth Bay for the night. Originally it had been intended that *Glory* would rejoin the

Mediterranean Fleet, but by early 1951 the war in Korea had become a major commitment for British troops fighting alongside US and other United Nations led forces. It had been decided to send her out to the Far East to relieve *Theseus* off Korea. On Friday 26 January *Glory* weighed anchor and set course for the Mediterranean and a non-stop passage to Malta. After steaming through a very rough Bay of Biscay, by the time she had reached southern Portugal the weather had become warmer and the seas calmer. During the forenoon of 2 February she arrived in Grand Harbour and secured alongside Hamilton Wharf in French Creek. For three days the carrier embarked the personnel and stores of the 14th Carrier Air Group, consisting of the Sea Furies of 804 and the

During 22 March 1951, on her way to the Far East, *Glory* made her southbound transit of the Suez Canal.

Once she had reached warmer waters "Hands to Bathe" became a regular feature of days at sea.

Fireflies of 812 Squadron. On 5 February she left harbour to embark the aircraft from Hal Far, and to start a six-week intensive work-up and training period. For the remainder of February and the first two weeks of March, apart from the occasional weekend in Grand Harbour, the carrier remained at sea with both the ship's company and the squadrons undergoing a rigorous training programme. However, with the Mediterranean Fleet having started its spring cruise, when she did get into harbour Glory's ship's company had Valletta to themselves.

At midnight on Sunday 18 March, with the work-up successfully completed, Glory slipped quietly out of Grand Harbour and set course for Port Said, escorted by the destroyer Gravelines. After spending eight hours moored in Port Said Harbour, during which

Glory moored off Aden's Steamer Point. The barren rocks of The Crater behind Steamer Point show the inhospitable nature of Aden. Usually 24 hours in port was more than long enough for most members of the ship's company.

Looking very smart in their tropical whites, the ship's company at Divisions in the Indian Ocean. The escorting destroyer is *Gravelines*.

shore leave was granted and the local bars and the Simon Artz department store did a roaring trade, the carrier entered the Suez Canal at just before midnight on 21 March. Next afternoon she cleared Port Suez and set course for Aden, which was reached during the morning of 26 March. The stay in Aden lasted for just 24 hours, which was quite long enough for everyone. As she steamed through the breakwater bound for Singapore, the Royal Marines Band played "Slow Boat to China", a very appropriate choice as she headed east. When she was off the coast of Ceylon the ship took part in training manoeuvres with the East Indies Fleet and it was during these exercises, on 3 April, that the first flying accident of the commission took place. *Glory* was in company with the cruiser *Mauritius* and destroyers of the East Indies Fleet, and a serial of two Sea Furies and four Fireflies was being launched by catapult. Unfortunately, the last Firefly crashed into the sea, but *Gravelines* was quick off the mark and her sea boat recovered the crew, Commissioned Pilot J. T. Griffiths and the observer, Sub-Lieutenant J. S. Kendall, and returned them safely to the carrier. Three days later *Glory* arrived in Singapore and secured alongside the naval base.

Glory's visit to Singapore lasted for just over 24 hours before she was at sea again and bound for Hong Kong where, after flying off the aircraft to Kai Tak,

she arrived at midday on 11 April. During her eight days in Hong Kong the opportunity was taken to carry out a large programme of self-maintenance. Stores, ammunition and Avgas were embarked. Ashore the ten Sea Furies, six Fireflies and the Sea Otter were able to carry out flying practice, although this was somewhat restricted by fog. In order to avoid the possibility of the ship's departure from Hong Kong being delayed, during 19 April all the aircraft were embarked from lighters. Next day, at 0830, escorted by the destroyer *Constance*, *Glory* left Hong Kong. After passing Lei Yue Mun, thick fog was encountered which did not lift until about 1300, when course was altered to the south-east, clear of the coast. As soon as weather permitted there was an afternoon of flying practice, on conclusion of which *Constance* returned to Hong Kong and *Glory* set course for Japan. That night, at the southern end of the Formosa Channel, thick fog again descended and with visibility down to 100 yards, speed was reduced to 12 knots. For two days the thick blanket of fog prevented any flying. During the forenoon of 21 April the carrier rendezvoused with the destroyer *Consort*. As no flying was possible the opportunity was taken to carry out a full-scale damage control exercise, and a gas alarm was also exercised which necessitated closing the whole ship down. Finally, at 1040 on 23 April *Glory* and *Consort*

Flying operations in the Indian Ocean as *Glory* steams east.

entered the swept channel at the Japanese port of Sasebo on the western side of Kyushu, and the carrier secured to No 21 buoy in the harbour.

The port of Sasebo, with its sophisticated ship repair and maintenance facilities, was the responsibility of Rear-Admiral W. G. Andrewes, Flag Officer, Second-in-Command, Far East Station, and acted as the forward operating base for units of the fleet involved in the Korean War. Also in harbour was *Glory's* sister ship *Theseus* which had just completed a seven-month tour of duty off Korea. Her officers and men were all extremely pleased to see *Glory*, for they were waiting to start their passage home, via Hong Kong, Singapore and Suez! Two days after *Glory's* arrival, when all essential stores had been transferred from *Theseus* to *Glory* (including the former's US Navy Sikorsky S51 helicopter, its pilot, Lt P O'Mara USN, and crewman CPO Frindley) *Theseus* left harbour to start her voyage home. Her involvement in the Korean War was over.

Glory's arrival in the Korean theatre of war had coincided with the joint North Korean and Chinese spring offensive, which started on 22 April, and which involved British Army units, including the Gloucestershire Regiment and the brand new Centurion tanks of the 8th Hussars. It was the start of the Battle of the Imjin, at which the Gloucesters' gallant stand on "Hill 235" at Solma-ri, south of the Imjin River, delayed the enemy advance for three days. Although the offensive gained some ground, the gallant defence by the Gloucesters and the covering fire of the tanks of the 8th Hussars allowed for an orderly retreat and the South Korean capital Seoul did not fall. In May the UN forces were able to regain the offensive and retake all the lost ground.

Glory's first Korean patrol began on Thursday 26 April, when she left Sasebo in company with the destroyers *HMAS Warramunga*, *HMCS Athabaskan*, *HMCS Nootka* and *HMCS Huron*, to steam to the operational area off Clifford Island, in the Yellow Sea,

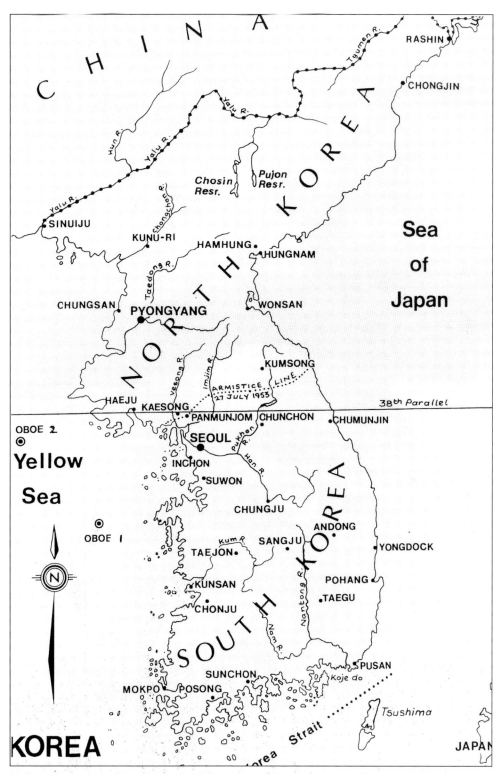

A map of Korea showing the main operating area off the west coast of South Korea, between points "Oboe 1" and "Oboe 2".

Briefing aircrews prior to a sortie over Korea, allowing last minute details to be resolved before launching.

A Sea Fury takes to the air just seconds after a catapult launch. Two "badgers" run towards the catapult to prepare it for the next launch.

west of Kunsan. For the first few days of the patrol poor visibility caused by fog, low cloud and rain, prevented any flying until the afternoon of Saturday 28 April when the first of 15 sorties was able to take off. During this first operational period, sorties were kept to a number compatible with unhurried arming up by inexperienced ground teams. The loss of Sea Fury 103 and its pilot, Lt E. P. L. Stephenson, on the first day was a bitter blow. Lt Stephenson was flying on a combat air patrol (CAP) when, after following his leader through a cloud layer at between 800 and 1,500 feet, he lost control and dived into the sea. The destroyer *Huron* was detached to search the area, but all she could find was a wheel and a large oil slick. That afternoon *Huron* came alongside the carrier to transfer Lt Barrow RCN, who was suffering from acute appendicitis and needed urgent medical attention. In the evening he was operated upon in the sickbay, but post-operational complications set in and the patient's condition deteriorated. Eventually he was transferred to *Warramunga* for passage to Sasebo as immediate hospital treatment was considered to be his best hope for survival.

Glory's aircraft operated in close support of the UN ground forces ashore, interrupting the Communist supply routes, acting as spotters for bombarding ships, and continually reconnoitring the coast to ensure that no supplies reached the Communist forces by sea. Once operations were well under way an average of 50 sorties were flown daily, approximately two thirds of them being Sea Furies armed with cannon and eight 60lb rockets, the remainder being Fireflies, with cannon and two 500lb bombs. Owing to the large number of aircraft onboard, there was always a large deck park so the planes were catapulted, or flown off by rocket-assisted-take-off-gear (RATOG), which was quite an awe-inspiring sight. Flying would begin at dawn, and strikes would then take off at approximately two-hourly intervals until sunset. As soon as a strike sortie and CAP were airborne the previous one landed, and there was then considerable activity refuelling and re-arming before they were ready to take off again. So intensive was the activity in preparing aircraft for sorties that the Royal Marines Band was pressed into assisting the ground crews with re-arming, and they soon became as efficient with a rocket jigging machine as they were with trombones, flutes and piccolos. By day the ship's company would be at Defence Stations, and at night the ship would go to Cruising Stations, with all the defensive armament fully manned. Although enemy aircraft rarely ventured close to the naval Task Elements, to give the AA gunners some routine practice, whenever *Glory* was nearing Sasebo at the end of a patrol American aircraft would fly over towing targets. On average during a patrol *Glory* would use some 250 bombs, 1,500 rockets and 100,000 rounds of cannon ammunition.

On 2 May, *Glory's* aircraft co-ordinated their air strikes with a North Korean anti-Communist guerrilla organization, code-named "Leopard", and the Sea Furies targeted large buildings in the Haeju area. However, after the attack a Sea Fury flown by Lt (E) P. Barlow, developed engine trouble and the pilot force-landed in a coastal stream north of the bomb line in enemy territory. Fortunately he was swiftly rescued by a US helicopter and next day he was delivered back to *Glory* none the worse for his adventure. There is no doubt that the expeditious rescue was a real boost to aircrew morale, and his aircraft was strafed and set on fire to prevent it falling into enemy hands. Three days after this incident the inner gun of a Sea Fury being flown by Commissioned Pilot P. McKerral blew up, tearing three feet off the leading edge of the plane's wing. Fortunately, the pilot was able to land the aircraft ashore safely, and a technician was put ashore to carry out temporary repairs, enabling the plane to be flown back to the ship that same afternoon. Next day, on 6 May, a Firefly developed an overspeeding engine, but again the pilot was able to land his plane ashore safely.

Glory's first patrol ended during the evening of 6 May and she was able to set course for Sasebo, where she arrived the following day for a short break. Captain Colquhoun was able to report that his carrier's first operations had been: "...most interesting and operations proceeded fairly smoothly once US signal procedure and terminology had been absorbed. Such phrases as, 'my crystal is blurred', meaning, 'my radar is not working', and, 'my wind gauge is sick', meaning, 'my annometer is out of order', are now readily understood by all." As a run ashore Sasebo was always more popular than Kure, although the town, in the words of one member of the ship's company, looked, "derelict and decrepit, with shops little more than shacks, and houses all monotonous, unpainted, drab wooden bungalows, with dingy grey slate roofs. In the main street the shops opened straight out on to the narrow roadway, looking like a cross between an Indian bazaar and one of the back streets of Port Said." There was, however, a fleet canteen for Commonwealth servicemen and, it was said, an interesting line in striptease shows could be found in the town. For those who wished to travel further afield there was a pearl farm and a china factory, both of which were happy to open their doors to organized groups of servicemen, to whom they would sell their products at a "very special price".

Glory's first break between patrols was brief. On Thursday 10 May, together with *Huron*, she left Sasebo to head for the operational area off Clifford Island, where she relieved *USS Bataan*. Flying operations began the next day and Fireflies attacked bridges at Wontan and Yonan, enemy troops in the area from the Han River to Chinnampo, the port for Pyongyang, and villages which intelligence reports indicated were being used by hostile forces. Throughout the following days aircraft from *Glory* attacked supply lines from Pyongyang southwards to Haeju, destroying or damaging buildings and transport and, east of Haeju, exploding ammunition dumps and starting large fires. Railway tunnels were targeted by Sea Furies, which approached them in shallow dives, firing their rockets

at the tunnel ends in order to destroy rolling stock or stores secreted inside. Monday 14 May was a replenishment day and at 1100 *Glory* went alongside *RFA Wave Premier* to refuel, an operation which lasted until 1440. However, at 1422, one of the carrier's refuelling personnel, Able Seaman J. McPherson, caught his foot in a bight of rope and, clad in oilskins and sea boots, he was thrown overboard. As it happened the ship's helicopter was airborne with a naval photographer taking newsreel pictures of the replenishment operation. The pilot, Lt O'Mara, noticed men running aft along the carrier's flight deck and spotted lifebuoys which had been thrown into the sea. The helicopter was quickly over the struggling McPherson who, in his heavy clothing, was almost exhausted. In order to rescue him the photographer, Petty Officer E. J. King, volunteered to jump into the sea where he was able to support the unfortunate rating and assist him in securing the sling. He was quickly hauled up to the helicopter's door, but was so exhausted that he was unable to pull himself inside. So, with both men dangling from the sling they were flown back to *Glory* where they were lowered safely on to the flight deck. Although carried out by a US Navy helicopter and pilot, it was the Royal Navy's first SAR (Search And Rescue) rescue by a ship's helicopter.

A aerial view of *Glory* operating off Korea. The planeguard helicopter hovers off the starboard side.

Although operations by *Glory's* aircraft had generally been successful and the morale of the aircrew was high, it was clear that ashore the enemy troops were quickly repairing bridges and filling in bomb craters. Pilots were also reporting an increase in enemy small arms fire and light flak. It was the latter which, on 15 May, was to result in the loss of another Sea Fury. That day a hanging mist and rain had delayed the start of flying operations and, in the event, only one sortie was flown. One of the four Sea Furies on CAP duties encountered heavy flak in the area north of Pyongyang and was hit, sustaining a serious oil leak. Fortunately, the pilot, Lt J. A. Winterbottom, managed to ditch his aircraft in the sea close to friendly islands and he swam to a sampan which took him ashore. That evening a helicopter from the US Navy's *LST 799* rescued him and next day, having suffered only minor facial injuries, he was returned to *Glory*. That same day a friendly junk belonging to a South Korean family was sunk by one of *Glory's* aircraft. The main causes of this regrettable incident were a navigational error by the pilot, the fact that the vessel was not flying a flag and the lack of normal friendly waving by its crew.

Although poor weather conditions limited flying operations on 16 May, during the last three days of the patrol 155 sorties were flown by the carrier's aircraft. Throughout this period the Fireflies bombed and rocketed bridges and villages, as well as strafing ammunition convoys. They also undertook spotting duties for the cruisers *Ceylon* and *Kenya* when they were carrying out shore bombardments. On Saturday 19 May a Firefly being flown by Lt R. Williams and Aircrewman 1 K. L. J. Sims, was hit by enemy rifle fire which caused a serious leak in the plane's coolant system. The pilot managed to get the aircraft to the shoreline, but he was forced to ditch in just three feet of water, some 70 miles north of *Glory*. The helicopter was quickly dispatched to the scene and two and a half hours later it returned both aircrew members to the ship. Lt Williams was unhurt, but his observer had received two bullet wounds to his left arm and was rushed to the sickbay for an immediate operation. It was clear that small arms fire was making low-level attacks more hazardous, and pilots were instructed to try and avoid flying too low. As it happened that incident marked the end of *Glory's* patrol and that evening, after handing over to *USS Bataan*, she left

Arming a Firefly with 3-inch rocket projectiles, fitted with 60lb warheads.

the operational area for Sasebo - which she reached the next day. With a recurring defect in one of her stern glands, the carrier's speed had been reduced to just 18 knots and there were also minor defects in her catapult and barrier, all of which meant a maintenance period and a spell of dry docking would be required.

Glory's stay at Sasebo lasted for two weeks and during this period she spent four days in the Sasebo Shipbuilding Company's No 3 dry dock. It was at this time that the ship's company were notified of a signal from the Admiralty which left them in no doubt as to the long-term future of their stay in Far Eastern waters. It said: "It has been found desirable to give aircrews and ships' companies of aircraft carriers a period of rest after six months of service in Korean waters. If the war in Korea continues, *HMS Glory* will then require some relief in October, and to effect this, while avoiding even a temporary reduction in the British Commonwealth contribution to the United Nations' forces in Korea, the Australian Government

Glory's officers and ship's company pose for the traditional photographs. Every inch of deck space is used....

H.M.S.GLORY~KOREA 1951

H.M.S.GLORY~KOREA 1951

A Sea Fury armed with two 500lb bombs. The aircraft's starboard drop tank has been modified to take a reconnaissance camera which was used for target analysis.

has generously agreed to make *HMAS Sydney* available for Korean service for three months from October." It was apparent from this signal that *Glory* would not be able to return to the UK, and rumours about the location of her temporary break from Korea abounded. For the time being, however, she had to return to sea for a further series of patrols. On 3 June 1951 she left Sasebo to again relieve *USS Bataan* in the operational area.

Flying operations began next day with the aircraft attacking junks which were suspected of delivering war materials to the ports of Hanchon and Kumsan-ni, but at 1800 on 4 June, when returning from the final sortie of the day, Lt P. A. L. Watson's Sea Fury suffered an engine failure. He was able to ditch the plane successfully in the Cho-do Channel, and was rescued by the frigate *Black Swan*. Next day, 5 June, flying operations were again under way at dawn, but an early catapult failure meant that the first range was launched by RATOG. After attacking junks, a railway bridge at Yonan and troop concentrations at three villages where buildings were destroyed, a serial of six Sea Furies and four Fireflies returned at 1445 to land on. One of the aircraft, flown by Pilot S. W. E. Ford, had received some damage during his armed reconnaissance mission and it is thought his engine suffered a loss of coolant after being hit by enemy fire. After a

wave-off during his final approach Ford's aircraft suffered an engine failure and he ditched ahead of the ship. Although the ditching was well executed, as the plane hit the water it pitched forward and sank very quickly, before the pilot could escape. Fortunately, an observer was not being carried at the time. During 6 June the Furies flew armed reconnaissance missions, and buildings and barges in the Chinnampo area were attacked, while targets closer to the coast were bombed by the Fireflies. At 1317 on 7 June, a Firefly flown by Lt R. E. Wilson and his observer, Sub-Lieutenant R. Shipley, was hit by flak and was forced to ditch near to Kirin-do Island. In this case both men were picked up by a shore-based helicopter and taken to Paengyong-do, from where *Glory's* helicopter was able to pick them up. In another incident a Sea Fury, whose brakes had been damaged by enemy fire, taxied into another aircraft which was in the park, damaging them both. That day the 2,000th deck landing since the start of the commission took place.

On 9 June the Task Element replenished from *RFA Wave Premier*, but the aviation fuel supplied by the tanker was found to be contaminated by a very fine black powder. Despite filtering it through a chamois leather it was impossible to remove the residue and a subsequent investigation found that the cast iron discharge pipes in *Wave Premier* were corroded.

A Firefly being launched with RATOG. This method was used if the ship's catapult was unserviceable.

Although reports appeared in British newspapers that the fuel had been sabotaged, these were quickly denied. At 1123 on 11 June, whilst *Glory's* aircraft were returning from an armed reconnaissance mission, an enemy twin jet aircraft was spotted high over Choppeki Point. It was the first sighting of an enemy aircraft during the carrier's patrols, but it made no attempt to interfere with *Glory's* planes. Although flying operations were able to continue, the contaminated fuel was pumped back to *Wave Premier* and *Glory*,

in company with *Cockade* and *Constance*, set course for Sasebo where she arrived the following day. Once in port the carrier embarked clean aviation fuel from *RFA Green Ranger*, and after only six hours departed for Kure where she arrived on Friday 15 June.

During the six-day visit to Kure there was an intensive programme of maintenance to carry out and the Harima Shipbuilding Works was used to provide assistance. Although the town was smaller than Sasebo, the ship's company found it more colourful

A Sea Fury on a bombing mission over Korea.

and with a better and cheaper shopping centre. According to one member of the ship's company it was more "permanent looking", and it was not long before the mess decks started to fill up with silks, musical cigarette boxes, sets of cultured pearls, damascene work and amazingly ingenious small clockwork animals. Kure also boasted a large grass playing field, and on most days one would see cricket being played at one end, football at the other and a game of hockey in between. Near Kure, on the island of Miyajima, was one of the biggest and most famous of Shinto shrines with its ornamental gateway built into the sea. The 1,000-year-old monument proved a great attraction for organized trips from the carrier.

During the forenoon of Thursday 21 June, both *Glory* and *Cockade* left Kure and, steaming via the Shimonoseki Channel, returned to the operational area, where *Glory* again relieved *USS Bataan*. At 0600 on 22 June, Rear-Admiral Scott-Moncrieff, who had succeeded Admiral Andrewes as FO2 FES, embarked by jackstay from the frigate *Cardigan Bay* and three-quarters of an hour later flying operations began. For four days Glory's aircraft carried out their bombing and armed reconnaissance missions over North Korean positions and during that time they clocked up their 1,000th operational sortie. On 24 June Admiral Scott-Moncrieff transferred to *Alacrity* and three days later when flying ceased *Glory* replenished from *RFA Green Ranger*. Although the weather remained fine for this fourth patrol, the ship's helicopter was unserviceable, and in order to be as close as possible to a land-based helicopter the carrier operated some 30 miles further north than usual. On 25 June four Sea Furies which were on an armed reconnaissance mission were attacked by four USAF F-80 Shooting Stars. Fortunately the Sea Furies were able to take evasive action and suffered no damage, but with black and white bands round fuselage and mainplanes, it was difficult to understand how they had been mistaken for the enemy.

At 1430 on Thursday 28 June a serial of six Fireflies and six Sea Furies was launched to carry out bombing raids on a military barracks installation in the Chinnampo area. An hour later when they were over their target, Firefly WB 308, being flown by Lt J. H. Sharp and Aircrewman G. B. Wells, was shot down immediately after they had released their bombs. The aircraft caught fire and crashed to the ground in flames, killing both crew members. On 29 June there was a very regrettable incident when, between Uridi and Taenko-To islands, a Sea Fury sank what turned out to be a friendly junk. The vessel was being used by a top secret intelligence organization code-named "Salamander" and as well as its three crew members, it was carrying two intelligence agents, all of whom were killed. Unfortunately the junk had failed to make any recognition signal, despite the fact that the plane had fired a warning burst and had allowed a further one and a half minutes elapse before attacking. It transpired that so secret was the "Salamander" organization that even Captain Colquhoun was unaware of its existence. It was agreed that the pilot had acted entirely within his briefing. However, as a result of the incident, it was decided that carrier-borne aircraft would not attack any craft within a specific area. Next day, at 1435 on Saturday 30 June, when Sea Fury 113 was being launched from the catapult, the launching bridle became detached and the aircraft ditched just ahead of the ship. The pilot, Sub-Lieutenant Howard, managed to escape and although bruised, was successfully rescued by *Cockade*. The catapult, however, was rendered unserviceable for the remainder of the patrol, and all future sorties were launched by RATOG, which doubled the arming-up tasks. The patrol ended at 0708 on Tuesday 3 July when, after a choppy passage on the edge of typhoon "Kate", *Glory* secured to No 18 buoy in Sasebo Harbour.

During the carrier's seven days in harbour all aircrew were granted five days' station leave, which they spent at Asokanko, a half-day's journey from Sasebo, in an hotel some 3,000 feet up on the edge of a volcanic crater in one of Japan's national parks. The building had been designed and constructed to house competitors in what should have been the 1940 Olympic Games, which were to have been held in Japan. Following the outbreak of war in Korea it had been taken over by the US Army. Its facilities included an open-air swimming pool, sulphur baths and tennis courts, all much appreciated by the visitors. Back at Sasebo the maintenance work on *Glory* included repairs to the catapult and the replenishment of stores, fuel and ammunition.

Glory's fifth patrol began on Tuesday 10 July when, in company with *Consort* and *Huron*, she left Sasebo to return to the operational area. Next day *Nootka* and *USS Moore* joined the screen, although fog and low cloud delayed the start of flying. During the first five days of operations buildings, junks and troop concentrations were attacked. The aircraft were also dispatched to locate and fix the exact position of an almost intact MiG-15 fighter, which was reported by intelligence to be lying off the west coast of Korea, over 100 miles behind enemy lines, having been shot down two days earlier by US forces. The first confirmation of this top-secret Soviet jet came from Lt W. R. Hart during the morning of 11 July, when he spotted the aircraft's tail and the position was fixed as Lat 39°-12'N/Long 125°-22'E. Bad weather in the area prevented further reconnaissance until 13 July, when Lt D. A. McNaughton sighted the rest of the plane about 100 yards further inshore and it was decided to attempt recovery of the wreck.

HMS Cardigan Bay (Captain W. L. M. Brown OBE DSC RN) was given the task of retrieving the machine, which was to prove very difficult given the fact that it was in shallow water and could only be approached by shallow water craft. Led by *Cardigan Bay*, a South Korean motor launch and a US Navy landing craft were guided through the treacherous channels between sand banks, which were only a few miles from the enemy coast. Overhead, aircraft from *Glory* provided air cover. *Cardigan Bay's* ship's divers, led by Lt M. Ross, assisted by US Navy personnel, got to work lifting the wreck, while PO Bill Feltham, wearing a shallow water diving set without a suit, dived into deeper holes to try to locate further wreckage. As the task could not be completed on one tide, during the night *Glory's* aircraft were relieved by fighters from *USS Sicily*, and next day the MiG was finally recovered. Before leaving the area both *Cardigan Bay* and *Sicily* bombarded enemy positions and achieved some direct hits. The recovery of the Soviet MiG-15 was one of the West's most valuable intelligence coups of the 1950s, and of *Glory's* part in the operation Captain Brown reported: "The part played by the aircraft from *Glory* in locating and marking the crashed fighter contributed materially to the success of the recovery, and the presence of low-flying close air support provided by the aviators from *Glory* and *Sicily* was of the greatest moral value to the recovery teams."

Meanwhile, on board *Glory* the intense flying operations continued with 418 sorties being flown. Over 130 tons of explosives were launched at enemy store dumps, military buildings, bridges and transport. On Monday 16 July flying operations were limited by low cloud, but at 1150 a flight of six Sea Furies and five Fireflies were launched on bombing raids at targets south of the town of Sariwan. Unfortunately, Firefly WB 380, flown by Lt R. Williams and Sub-Lieutenant I. R. Shepley, was hit by flak and it crashed to the ground in flames. Next day, at 0930, a flight of six Sea Furies and five Fireflies was launched on a mission to strike at targets in the Chinnampo area, but Sea Fury VW 661, flown by Lt Hart, was hit by anti-aircraft fire and he ditched his aircraft close to the island of Taechong-Do. He was promptly picked up by a South Korean frigate, and *Constance* was detached to collect him. At 09.17 on 18 July Lt P. S. Davis, was forced to ditch his Sea Fury VX 609 into the sea, and with no ships in the vicinity, he had to spend one and a half hours in the sea before being rescued but, apart from suffering from mild exposure and mild pneumonia, he was unhurt. Just over two and a half hours later, at 1155, Sea Fury VW 573, flown by Commissioned Pilot T. W. Sparke, was hit by flak while strafing targets near Sariwan and crashed in flames. On 19 July, a Firefly piloted by Lt J. R. C. Johnson, was returning from an anti-submarine patrol when, after a late wave-off, he hit the round down and bounced high. Fortunately he managed to increase his engine speed to clear the forward deck park, but his port wheel was damaged by hitting the turning propeller of a Sea Fury, which gave the pilot of that aircraft a surprise. He made a well-executed wheels-up belly landing. Both Lt Johnson and his observer Sub-Lieutenant R. J. P. Bates were uninjured. Friday 20 July saw the final full day of operations and next day *Glory* set course for Kure. Although thick fog was encountered in the Island Sea, the weather was bright and sunny when, on Sunday 22 July, the carrier secured to a buoy in Kure Harbour.

During the stay at Kure, which was scheduled to last for seven days, Captain Colquhoun went ashore for medical treatment. Down below in the main machinery spaces, with notice for steam set at 24 hours, the engineering department had opened up two of the main boilers to carry out a boiler clean, which was a very hot and dirty job. However, no sooner had they started the task than the senior UN delegate at the peace talks, which had started on 10 July at Kaesong, requested a show of force in the Han estuary area,

A formation of Fireflies on a strike mission.

close to Kaesong, and both *Glory* and *USS Sicily* were ordered to concentrate air operations in the area. During the early hours of Wednesday 25 July, orders were received to prepare *Glory* for sea immediately and to sail that forenoon. There then followed an extremely strenuous night as liberty men were recalled and the engineers worked hard to close up the boilers and raise steam which, to their credit, they managed to do in just seven hours.

At 0918 on 25 July *Glory* slipped her moorings and steamed out to sea and an hour later Captain Colquhoun, who was on sick leave, flew back on board by helicopter. As for the ship's company, he was able to report on their efforts thus: "The engine room department, especially, are to be congratulated on their efforts, considering the ship was at 24 hours' notice for steam and a boiler clean was in progress. None of the ship's company missed the ship on sailing through leave-breaking." A number of *Glory's* pilots were on local leave and others were on duty at an RAAF base near Iwakuni, and they were all returned to the ship by helicopter whilst she was en route to the operational area. One of the escorts, *HMCS Huron*,

had to remain behind in Kure, for a third of her ship's company were on local leave and could not be easily recalled. After steaming through the Shimonoseki Channel *Glory* was joined by *HMCS Cayuga*, and next morning she met *USS Moore*, *USS Renshaw*, *HMAS Warramunga* and *HMNLS Van Galen*. Later in the day the force joined *USS Sicily* and her escorts. The first strikes were scheduled to be launched at 1800, but bad weather caused the cancellation of all flying. No air strikes could be flown until the following afternoon, when bombing missions were flown to the Chinnampo area. On Saturday 28 July, following an accident on *Sicily's* flight deck, one of her Corsairs was diverted to *Glory*. A US Navy landing control officer was transferred to *Glory* by helicopter and he succeeded in bringing in the first US Navy plane to land on *Glory* during the commission. That the landing was made without incident proved the adaptability of the joint Anglo-American carrier force, and *Glory's* Landing Control Officers gained a great deal of valuable experience through watching their opposite number in action. Although landing techniques were standard procedure in both navies, the US aircraft appeared to be "cut" at a greater height. The Corsair was successfully catapulted off later that day. At 1930 that evening the whole Task Element assumed First Degree Readiness when *USS Renshaw* reported a submarine contact. A number of depth charge and hedgehog attacks were made and oil slicks were seen to rise to the surface. However, after maintaining a close watch on the area for 48 hours nothing more was seen, and the conclusion was that the echo had come from a large wreck in the area.

During the middle watch on Monday 30 July, with strong winds blowing and high seas, there was another alarm aboard *Glory* when a lifebuoy sentry reported a commotion on a weather deck on the port side of the ship. A search of all mess decks accounted for all unoccupied hammocks and camp beds. The disturbance was eventually traced to the ship's Maltese cat which was prowling the area at the time! Later that day the carrier encountered her first severe gale in the Yellow Sea, which was closely followed by thick fog which restricted flying operations. On 1 August the Task Element fuelled from *RFA Wave Chief*, and for the remainder of the patrol poor weather conditions continued to affect flying. However, some spotting missions were flown as ships of the Task Element bombarded targets in the Han River estuary. Air cover was also provided for *Mounts Bay* when she reported being attacked by an enemy plane, which was described as a twin-engined jet. Although a bomb was dropped close to the escort screen, no damage was caused and the enemy aircraft disappeared into the mist.

Some indication of the poor weather and visibility can be gauged from one incident which took place during the afternoon of Thursday 2 August. In torrential rain, with visibility down to just 400 yards, two Sea Furies which were returning from CAP duties over ships in the Han Estuary were airborne for three and three quarter hours before they were able to land on. In the end, the boiler rooms were ordered to make thick black smoke to guide the planes home. This obviously worked, for at 1415 they landed safely. Finally, at 2000 that day, *Glory* left the operating area and set course for Sasebo. During the patrol 312 sorties had been flown, some 40,000 rounds of 20mm ammunition, over 1,000 rocket projectiles and over 100, 500lb bombs had been fired at North Korean personnel and installations. The weather during the patrol

A Firefly over Korea.

had been the worst encountered by *Glory* in the Yellow Sea, with severe gales or thick fog arriving with little notice. Happily, however, there had been no casualties.

After five days at Sasebo, during which time she embarked spares and replacements which had arrived in her sister ship *Warrior*, *Glory* left the port with *Concord* at 0830 on 10 August and set course for Kure. Next morning, she anchored off Iwakuni for a few hours in order to embark 11 replacement aircraft, which were shipped out to the carrier by lighters. By 1335 she was at last alongside No 8 pontoon at Kure, where the ship's company were able to enjoy a run ashore after a busy patrol.

Glory and *Concord* left Kure on Monday 13 August to proceed, via the Van Dieman Strait, to the operating area. Once again poor weather conditions limited flying operations, but on 15 and 16 August offensive missions were flown and spotting was also carried out for bombarding units in the Han River area. During operations on 15 August an aircraft was hit by flak and the pilot, Lt R. F. Hubbard, was forced to land at Paengyong Island. The US destroyer *Naifeh* was immediately detached to land air maintenance ratings on the island, and next day the plane was flown back to the carrier. Meanwhile, two more aircraft from *Glory* were having problems. The first, flown by Lieutenant D. A. McNaughton, had taken a hit from a .303 bullet through its oil system and had been forced to land at Kimpo. The other, which had also force-landed nearby, was undergoing a test flight when it crashed into a drainage ditch. This caused Captain Colquhoun to comment: "Unfortunately the condition of the runways at the forward airfields is by no means perfect."

At 1355 on 16 August the US destroyer *Wedderburn* came alongside to transfer a member of her ship's company who was suffering from appendicitis. After an operation on board *Glory* the patient recovered satisfactorily and was subsequently returned to his own ship. Next day FO2 FES transferred to *Glory* from the cruiser *Ceylon*, just in time for a passage south to avoid typhoon "Marge" which would dictate the carrier's movements for the remainder of the patrol. Later that day two of the older escorts were ordered to take shelter at Sasebo, and at noon on 18 August, with "Marge" not having made her intentions clear, *Glory* and her escorts steered for the Tsushima Strait. By that evening the weather reports were indicating that "Marge" was about to alter course, so in order to avoid being caught in the Strait they reversed their courses. The forenoon of Sunday 19 August found the force, now consisting of *Glory*, *Ceylon*, *Kenya*, three destroyers and two frigates, some 70 miles off the coast of China. With reports indicating that "Marge" was heading slowly for the Yellow Sea, two frigates and a destroyer, which were running short of fuel, were ordered to Inchon. *Glory* and the rest of the force then turned southward in order to work down west of the typhoon's centre. By this time the effects of "Marge" were being increasingly felt by the force and *Glory* was rolling heavily. At 0500 on 20 August, the carrier and her escorts were about 150 miles from the centre of the typhoon, steaming at 13 knots into 55 knot winds. With huge seas and visibility down to less than a mile due to spray and torrential rain *Glory* was rolling badly. At 1115 the force turned south-east and with conditions gradually improving, a decision was taken to head for Okinawa where the escorts could

refuel. Throughout the storm only one aircraft was slightly damaged when a bolt dislodged from the hangar deckhead and fell on it; one of *Glory's* boats was lost and the accommodation ladder was badly damaged. A few members of the ship's company suffered minor injuries and overall *Glory* had come through relatively unscathed.

On 21 August *Glory*, *Ceylon* and *Kenya* anchored at Buckner Bay, Okinawa, while the two accompanying destroyers went alongside to refuel and FO2 transferred to *Kenya*. At 0815 on Wednesday 22 August the force weighed anchor with a view to returning to the operational area, but with severe gales still blowing across the Yellow Sea (on 24 August) *Glory* was ordered to proceed to Kure, where she secured alongside No 4 berth.

A reconnaissance photograph of bridges which had been targeted by *Glory's* aircraft. Communist engineers soon repaired or rebuilt any bomb damage caused.

A close-up view of a demolished railway bridge.

After a seven-day break at Kure, *Glory* left on Friday 31 August, the same day that *HMAS Sydney* left Australia for Korean waters to relieve her. The weather during this operating period was consistently fine with good visibility. The cooler temperatures did a great deal to improve morale on board. Flying operations commenced on 2 September with junks, railway lines and villages being attacked. An average of over 50 sorties a day was maintained during seven full days of flying, and on 9 September a total of no less than 84 sorties was flown, which as Captain Colquhoun reported was, "...an achievement of which all concerned can be proud." The final event on that day involved 19 aircraft and when launched every plane in the ship was airborne. The results of the armed reconnaissance and bombing raids during this patrol were very good, which to a large extent was due to intelligence reports from guerrilla organization ashore. The discovery of a new junk landing place just south of the Chong Chon River was followed up by successful strikes on warehouses and the junks themselves.

On 2 and 3 September two aircraft suffered damage when making emergency landings ashore, but both were eventually recovered. During the last event on 9 September Firefly 203 was hit in the oil system by flak while carrying out a dive-bombing attack, but the pilot managed to land the aircraft on mud flats about a mile from the coast, in enemy territory south-east of Haeju. The ship's helicopter, piloted by CPO Babbit

USN, picked up the crew, but with a faulty fuel gauge in his own machine, ran short of fuel on the way back to the ship, and he then made an emergency landing on Pian-To Island. The destroyer *Sioux* came to their assistance, retrieving the rescued aircrew and delivering cans of avgas so that the helicopter was able to return to the ship at dawn; the ditched Firefly was subsequently destroyed by shore-based aircraft. During the evening of 9 September *USS Hanna* was detached to investigate a suspicious junk which was bound for Shantung. After taking off her crew *Hanna* set the cargo of petrol and oil ablaze with short-range weapons. As the burnt-out hulk was a danger to shipping, *Glory's* Fireflies sank it with depth charges. The carrier's patrol ended at 1630 on Tuesday 11 September, when she secured to her buoy in Kure Harbour once again.

After only a five-day break at Kure *Glory* left the port, in company with *Concord*, on Sunday 16 September, for the ninth and final patrol of her deployment. A few hours after sailing, however, "Jumbo", the mobile crane, which was being used to place a whaler in its sea stowage at the port after end of the flight deck, ran out of control, overrode the edge of the flight deck and fell on to the framework of the jib, dropping the whaler into the sea. In view of the vital importance of "Jumbo" during flying operations, both *Concord* and *Glory* returned to Kure where the crane was quickly exchanged for that belonging to the repair ship *Unicorn*. By 1615 the two ships were

산으로 피난하라!

큰길에서 물러가라!

군사작전에 휩쓸려들지말라!

즉 지않으려거든 곧!

Example of a leaflet which was dropped by *Glory's* aircraft over Communist-held areas, warning local people to keep clear of areas under attack by United Nations aircraft.

at sea once again and heading for the operational area, where they would rendezvous with *Cayuga*, *Sioux*, and US Navy's *Craig* and *Toledo*. The combined force, designated Task Group 95.9, was to operate off Korea's east coast.

Flying operations began on 18 September, when strikes on the North Korean port of Wonsan began and, in spite of low cloud over the target area, some very good results were achieved. Flak was not as intense as that encountered on the west coast, but this was attributed to airburst fire put up by *Toledo* just prior to the attack. That afternoon an elderly Russian Mk26 mine was spotted, and was exploded by gunfire from *Sioux*. Despite its decrepit appearance and covering of barnacles it still made an impressive explo-

sion. Flying on 19 September did not start until 1000 due to high winds, which forced Captain Colquhoun to move the ship south to a position abreast of the bomb line in order to obtain a lee. Then, after only two aircraft had been launched, the catapult failed and two strikes of 21 aircraft were launched by RATOG. With stocks of the rocket-assisted equipment running short, that evening *Glory* set course for Sasebo, where she arrived at 1450 on 20 September for a two and a half hour stay. That evening fresh RATOG equipment was embarked and at the same time, to cut down on the deck park, four Fireflies and one Sea Fury were transferred to *Unicorn* to reduce the size of the deck park. Leaving Sasebo at 1815 that day, *Glory* returned at 21 knots to the operating area and flying operations were resumed during the afternoon of 21 September. With no catapult all strike launches were made with the aid of RATOG, and to reduce rocket expenditure, free take-off was used for CAP aircraft. On 22 September the carrier rendezvoused with the cruiser *Belfast* and FO2 transferred to *Glory* for the day, rejoining *Belfast* by helicopter at 1800. During the launching of the 1130 strike, Firefly WB 309's RATOG failed to fire and the aircraft ditched ahead of the ship. Although it sank immediately, the pilot, Warrant Officer J. P. Hack, managed to escape and was picked up by helicopter within a few minutes. Sadly, the observer, Sub-Lieutenant R. G. A. Davey, was lost.

Flying operations on 23 and 24 September were almost entirely devoted to armed reconnaissance and strikes, with support being given to a guerrilla landing operation. At 1607 on 24 September the Sea Fury being flown by the Air Group Commander, Lt-Cdr S. J. Hall DSC, was hit by flak over Chinnampo and he was forced to ditch six miles north of Choppeki Point. He was in the water for 53 minutes before being rescued, cold but unhurt, by the ship's helicopter which refuelled at Paengyong-Do before returning to the ship. 25 September saw the last day of flying operations, with the first strikes being launched at 1028 and the last aircraft, a Firefly flown by Lt-Cdr Swanton, being recovered at 1808. By now there was a real "end-of-term" spirit on board and this last arrival was met by cheers from both "goofers" and flight deck personnel, a band and a good deal of foamite from fire extinguishers. Once flying was finished for the day, *Glory* and *Concord* left the operational area to set course for Matsoyama, where they anchored for a few hours before heading for Kure. At 0755 on Thursday 27 September *Glory* secured alongside No 4 berth at Kure where, on the opposite side of the pontoon, *Sydney* was waiting to take over from her.

For three days from her arrival at Kure *Glory* turned over her duties to *Sydney*, with Lt O'Mara USN and his helicopter crew receiving a rousing farewell. The value of the helicopter to the morale of the Air Group had been enormous. During the forenoon of Sunday 30 September, Vice-Admiral Sir Guy Russell, the C-in-C Far East Station, visited the ship and inspected Divisions, after which he congratulated everyone on their fine war record and wished them well for their forthcoming visit to Sydney, where *Glory* would undergo a refit. At 1630 that day, with *HMAS Anzac* as her escort, *Glory* left Kure and set course for Hong Kong.

During the passage, in the early hours of Tuesday 2 October, ERA 3 D. Dixon was lost overboard in what was thought to have been a suicide, which cast a shadow over the first few days away from the Korean war.

For the ship's company the arrival in Hong Kong on 3 October meant that, at last, they were able to proceed once again on all-night leave, and the locally enlisted Chinese ratings on board were pleased to be in their home port once again. *Glory* spent only 48 hours in Hong Kong before she set course for Singapore. After carrying out "Exercise Heave-To", during which RAF Brigand aircraft bombed splash targets towed by *Glory* and *Anzac*, she arrived at the naval base on 9 October. Once again, however, she remained in port for only 48 hours, which was long enough to embark stores, and on 11 October left Singapore bound for Australia. As she left harbour there was a fly-past by RAF Vampires and Meteors from RAF Tengah, and soon afterwards *Glory* was heading south. That evening she crossed the equator and at 1930, amid a display of pyrotechnics, King Neptune's Herald was received on board once again. The following day, Friday 12 October, despite wet and windy weather, Neptune held his court on the flight deck where he swiftly dealt with all defaulters.

At 0830 on Wednesday 17 October, after an extremely rough passage, *Glory* arrived in Fremantle,

This air dropped leaflet requests that local civilians help pro-UN guerrillas and downed UN airmen.

but stayed only long enough to refuel. By 1800 she was steaming into more gales as she set course for Sydney. On 22 October the aircraft were flown off to RANAS Nowra. After carrying out full-power trials in Jervis Bay, and an anti-submarine exercise with HM submarines *Thorough* and *Telemachus* outside Sydney Harbour, *Glory* secured alongside a berth at Garden Island, Sydney, at 0900 on 24 October. Ahead lay a refit for the ship while the ship's company could look forward to two months of rest and relaxation. They had earned it.

Chapter Seven

Return to Korea and a Mediterranean Sojourn: November 1951 - September 1952

While *Glory* underwent a two-month refit at Sydney her officers and men could enjoy some rest and relaxation. A few days after her arrival the Garden Island Dockyard was opened to the public to commemorate Trafalgar Day, an event which turned out to be very much like Navy Days at home. *Glory* was the main attraction, with some 12,000 visitors taking the opportunity to go aboard and look round. However, it was not long before the dockyard workers descended upon the ship and while she spent two weeks in the Captain Cook dry dock, her ship's company was granted 14 days' leave. Accommodation was no problem as the residents of Sydney were queuing to take the sailors into their homes and many men were able to see something of life in the outback, including the vast cattle and sheep stations. For some the bar opening hours, from 1000 to 1830, took some getting used to, but everyone enjoyed their runs ashore. The Royal Marines Band distinguished themselves by playing at the opening of the Davis Cup international tennis tournament, which

gained them some free tickets! The ship's company marched through Sydney's city centre, with the Lord Mayor taking the salute. Amid the Christmas celebrations, however, there were periods of mourning when a senior and a junior rating died, the latter after being hit by a moving train at Roseville Railway Station. On Christmas Eve the ship went to sea for just over seven hours, to carry out full-power and gun functioning trials, but by 1600 she was back alongside her berth at Woolloomooloo. Next day, in sweltering hot temperatures, the ship's company enjoyed a full Christmas dinner, complete with roast turkey and Christmas pudding.

On Wednesday 2 January 1952, with the Christmas and New Celebrations over, but with many hangovers still intact, *Glory* left Sydney to steam round to Jervis Bay where the Air Group landed on. On 4 January, after two days of deck landing practice, she returned to Sydney but only for the weekend. On Monday 7 January, with final farewells having been made, *Glory* was back at sea again and after four more days of deck

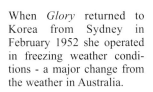

When *Glory* returned to Korea from Sydney in February 1952 she operated in freezing weather conditions - a major change from the weather in Australia.

Flight deck personnel dressed to withstand the elements - trying to remember those hot days in Sydney!

It was not only the bitter cold that disrupted flying operations. In this view a thick bank of fog rolls in towards *Glory*.

Often, before flying operations could begin, the flight deck had to be cleared of snow.

landing practice in the Jervis Bay area, the carrier set course for Fremantle and Singapore in company with the destroyer *Warramanga*. Again she remained at the former port just long enough to refuel, and spent three days at Singapore embarking winter clothing before proceeding to Hong Kong. She arrived on Wednesday 30 January. Waiting for her as she secured to No 2 buoy in the harbour was *HMAS Sydney*, and over the next two days the Australian carrier transferred stores and equipment, including the US Navy S-51 helicopter and its crew. With the handover completed, *Glory* left Hong Kong on 2 February to set course for Sasebo, where she arrived three days later. Her stay in the Japanese port was limited to just 16 hours, before she left for the operational area in the Yellow Sea, off Korea's west coast. During this deployment of five patrols her main task would be to provide air defences for the friendly islands of Sok-to, Cho-do, Pacngyong-do and other small islands. With flying operations having begun on 7 February, it must have seemed to her aircrews as though she had never been away and the squadrons were quickly averaging 50 sorties a day. Once again the aircraft were kept busy on bombing and armed reconnaissance missions in the area around Changyon and Haeju, and also spotting for the cruiser *Ceylon* and the destroyer *USS Porterfield*. During the patrol she lost only two aircraft, the first on 12 February when Lieutenant A. M.

Knight's Sea Fury was hit by flak and suffered a loss of oil pressure. Fortunately he was able to make a successful belly-landing at Paengyong, and was rescued later that day by *Glory's* helicopter. Next day another Sea Fury, flown by Lieutenant R. J. Overton, was hit after attacking a gun position and suffered a complete engine failure. He had enough height to be able to successfully ditch his aircraft in the sea close to the island of Cho-do, and after almost an hour in his dinghy he was picked up by the South Korean minesweeper *501*. On 14 February fog and poor visibility disrupted flying. The following day saw the final sorties before *Glory* set course for Sasebo, where she arrived on 16 February.

During her eight-day break at Sasebo two replacement Sea Furies were transferred by lighter from *Unicorn* and, in the freezing winter conditions, ammunition was embarked. On the evening of *Glory's* arrival Captain Colquhoun was taken ashore for medical treatment, and the ship's Executive Officer, Cdr R. L. Alexander DSO DSC, temporarily assumed command. Happily it was only for a few days and Captain Colquhoun rejoined the ship before she sailed. *Glory's* second patrol began at 0700 on Sunday 24 February, when she left Sasebo for the operational area where she relieved *USS Bairoko*. Flying operations began on 25 February, with rocket attacks on troop concentrations west of Chinnampo. Although

Glory and the destroyer *HMAS Bataan* replenish from *RFA Wave Premier*.

four aircraft were hit by small arms fire, all were able to return to the ship safely. Next day attacks were made on ammunition convoys and railway installations. It was during this patrol that the 5,000th deck landing was recorded, before on the last day of February, the carrier replenished from *RFA Green Ranger*. Flying operations began again on Saturday 1 March but once again poor visibility delayed the first strikes. However, once under way, sorties were launched against road and rail targets between Haeju and Changyon. At 1102 on Sunday 2 March, a Sea Fury which was returning from a combined CAP and armed reconnaissance mission lost oil pressure shortly before it was due to land on, but the pilot successfully ditched astern of the ship. Already airborne, the ship's helicopter rescued the pilot in exactly one minute - from ditching to being landed on the flight deck. On 4 March a catapult failure and a shortage of RATOG equipment reduced the number of sorties flown. Next day the ship's anti-aircraft gunners got some practice when they had to fire over the top of a local junk which was obstructing flying operations. The patrol ended on 5 March when *Glory* set course for Kure, where she arrived the next day.

Glory's third patrol began on Wednesday 12 March when, in company with *HMCS Nootka* and *USS Munro*, she sailed for the operating area. Once off Korea's west coast the carrier met the destroyer *Concord*, and Rear-Admiral Scott-Moncrieff, FO2 FES, transferred to *Glory* to watch flying operations. Once again the air strikes targeted enemy troops and communications, but on 15 March the ship suffered the only fatal casualty during this tour of duty. Lieutenant R. J. Overton, piloting a Sea Fury, had been strafing near Chinnampo, when he was hit by anti-aircraft fire and his aircraft crashed into a hillside near the Amgak Peninsular and exploded.

On Monday 17 March, with reports of an impending Communist attack on Sok-to Island, *Glory* mounted a full-scale air offensive on enemy targets in the area between Changyon and Chinnampo. During a day of intensive flying a total of 106 sorties were launched, which was a new record for a light fleet carrier. It was a magnificent effort by both aircrews and the maintenance personnel, who produced 100% serviceability during the day. From FO2, who witnessed flying operations that day, came the following signal, which was relayed to the C-in-C at Singapore: "I am very honoured to have been flying my flag in *Glory* when she achieved the remarkable daily total of 106 sorties. Well done all on board on this result and particularly the 14th Carrier Air Group. I have witnessed some first class airmanship and teamship today and I congratulate you all." The Admiralty sent the following signal: "Personal from Fifth Sea Lord. Congratulations on your fine century." For all aircrews and maintenance personnel Tuesday 18 March was a day of relaxation after their efforts the previous day, as *Glory* replenished from *RFA Green Ranger*. For the rest of the patrol poor weather conditions hampered flying. During the evening of Saturday 22 March, in gale force winds and torrential rain, the carrier left the operational area and at 1730 the next day, she secured to a buoy in Sasebo Harbour.

After an eight-day break and with the Fleet

Loading 20mm cannon shell into a Sea Fury.

Engineer, the Fleet Aviation and Fleet Gunnery Officers embarked, at 0700 on Monday 31 March *Glory* left Sasebo. Also on board was a Royal Navy Dragonfly helicopter and crew, which was to work on SAR duties with the US Navy machine. Lieutenant P. J. Edwards, the Assistant Operations Officer from *Ocean* was also embarked, who had to familiarize himself with operational policy and technique, in preparation for his own ship taking over from *Glory*. Accompanied by *HMCS Athabaskan* and *HMAS Warramunga*, *Glory* steamed in heavy seas and gale force winds. That night, however, with the escorts unable to maintain 18 knots to remain with the carrier, speed was reduced. At 0615 on 1 April, with the force still 52 miles south of its operating position (Lat 37°-28'N/Long 124°-12'E), flying operations commenced. Bombing missions were mounted on warehouses at Simpo and Kyomipo, air cover was provided for minesweeping operations in the Chinnampo Estuary and spotters were provided for *Ceylon* and *Chevalier* which were bombarding enemy gun positions on the Amgak Peninsular. Despite strong northwesterly winds and a heavy swell, some 59 sorties were flown that day. On 2 April when the catapult broke down several times, 54 sorties were achieved. On 3 April conditions became very cloudy, but visibility remained good and with a repaired catapult 59 sorties were flown in a good south-westerly wind. While approaching a target in the Taetan area a Firefly suffered a rough running engine and after jettisoning its bombs it subsequently made a wheels-up landing at Paengyong-do. The crew, who were unhurt, were rescued by the ship's helicopter which also flew experts to the scene to ascertain whether it would be possible to salvage the plane. The following day maintenance ratings took passage in *Abathaskan* and, having stripped the aircraft of important equipment, the Firefly was abandoned.

On 4 April, despite persistent coastal fog, 56 sorties were flown, including four in close air support of the 1st US Army Corps. Next day provided a break when *RFA Green Ranger* arrived with fuel, and at 0615 on 6 April flying operations against shore targets were resumed. That day the aircraft attacked railways and bridges, with one rail bridge north of Chinnampo being completely destroyed and another south-east of Sariwan being badly damaged. On 7 April sorties were flown in support of British troops of the 28th Commonwealth Brigade who, for the first time since the Great War, had a static defensive role. Two Fireflies took part in an island defence exercise over Sok-to Island. A Sea Fury was forced to land at Paengyong-do after engine failure, the pilot being ferried back to the ship by *Warramunga*. Fog prevented any flying on 8 April and operations recommenced in cloudy, but fine weather on the following day. During the day 61 sorties were flown, including more in support of the US Army. On completion of flying that day the popular US Navy helicopter and its crew flew ashore to Paengyong-do. The loan of the helicopter since the start of *Glory's* operations in Korea had been of the utmost value and it demonstrated the advantages of the helicopter over any other form of SAR aircraft. It had also proved invaluable in the distribution of mail and the occasional transfer of personnel. The three American crew members who had served in *Glory* had, in the words of Captain Colquhoun, "Operated their helicopter with great skill and zeal", and had been "very popular on board." At 1450 on Friday 11 April, when *Glory* secured at her berth in Kure at the end of the fourth patrol, she had by then steamed some 80,000 miles since the start of the commission, and over 6,000 deck landings had been made. She had even received a rather unusual visitor in the form of a Manchurian Crane, which stayed with the ship for 36 hours and appeared to enjoy life on the flight deck being fed kippers by the ship's company. He only departed in a huff after the helicopter began flying operations.

Glory's fifth and final patrol began at 0700 on Thursday 17 April, when she left Kure for the operational area and a rendezvous with the destroyers *HMCS Nootka* and *USS Munro*. During the first four days of the patrol fog reduced the number of sorties that could be flown, but once again troop concentrations and lines of communication were attacked. At 1530 on Tuesday 22 April two US Navy Avengers landed on board *Glory*, one of which was carrying the carrier's new commanding officer, Captain T. A. K. Maunsell RN. At 0900 next day Captain Maunsell took command of *Glory*, and at 1810, cheered by his ship's company, Captain Colquhoun transferred by jackstay to the New Zealand frigate *Rotoiti* for passage back to Sasebo. For *Glory* seven days of the patrol still remained.

On Thursday 24 April, *Glory's* aircraft were once

During a replenishment day *RFA Fort Sandusky* supplies 500lb bombs to *Glory*...

...and the bombs arrive on the flight deck.

Arming an aircraft with a 500lb bomb load.

again attacking the usual enemy targets, including lines of communication, troop concentrations and enemy-held villages. On 28 April poor visibility prevented flying until the afternoon, when attacks were mounted on convoys of stores and ammunition. At 1545 Sea Fury 103, flow by Sub-Lieutenant D. L. G. Swanson, suffered engine trouble whilst on a strafing attack near Pungsan. Fortunately he managed to reach the coast, where he ditched his aircraft south-west of Cho-do Island and took to his dinghy. After only 15 minutes he was rescued by a US helicopter and taken to the island before being returned safely to the ship.

Tuesday 29 April was *Glory's* final day of operations off Korea, with aircraft attacking villages and ammunition convoys. The final detail of four Fireflies took off at 1500 and once they had returned to the ship *Glory* set course for Sasebo, where she secured to No 18 buoy the next day. That same day *Ocean*, which was relieving *Glory* on station, arrived in Hong Kong from the Mediterranean.

Glory's second period of operations off Korea had been shorter than her first, but had been carried out in bitterly cold winter weather; now in Sasebo for her final 16-hour stay the abundance of cherry blossom ashore signalled the warmer weather. It had been decided that *Ocean*, which had joined the Mediterranean Fleet in August 1951, would relieve

Glory in order to give her a break from the intensive flying operations. This time there was to be a refit in Australia, for she had to take over *Ocean's* duties in the Mediterranean. Since leaving the UK in January 1951, *Glory* had steamed some 85,000 miles, had operated off four continents and had recorded more than 6,000 aircraft landings. During operations off Korea she had lost nine crew members and 27 aircraft, with 140 having been damaged. On the plus side, 24 aircrew members had been rescued after their planes had been shot down.

On Thursday 1 May *Glory* left Sasebo to set course for Hong Kong, where she arrived two days later to find both *Ocean* and the cruiser *Belfast* in harbour. During the next three days stores and aircraft were transferred by lighter to *Ocean*. Ashore sports teams from *Glory*, *Ocean* and *Belfast* took part in a number of tournaments. On Monday 5 May, the C-in-C FES visited *Glory* to say farewell, and at 0700 the next day the carrier left Hong Kong and set course for Malta.

There were brief stops at Singapore and Aden before, on 23 May, *Glory* began her transit of the Suez Canal. During a period at anchor in the Great Bitter Lake over 100 members of the ship's company were disembarked to spend a few weeks with the RAF in the Suez Canal Zone. At 2050 that day *Glory* herself passed through Port Said to head for Malta, where she

A Sea Fury which, having crashed into the barrier, has lost its wings and caught fire. A firesuitman is fighting the flames around the cockpit in order to help the pilot to escape and...

secured alongside Parlatorio Wharf on Monday 26 May. Within an hour of her arrival in Malta the ship was taken into dockyard hands and soon afterwards she was in the floating dry dock. Shortly after her arrival in Malta the personnel of the 14th Carrier Air Group, together with their remaining aircraft, were disembarked and transferred to *Theseus* for the passage home, where the Air Group was disbanded.

The spell in Malta made a pleasant change for the ship's company, and a few families were able to travel out to the island from the UK. On Thursday 3 July, with all the maintenance work having been completed, *Glory* and the destroyer *Chevron* left Grand Harbour for Port Said, where they arrived at 1530 on 6 July. Over a period of five hours a variety of stores and the personnel who had been left in Egypt in May were embarked, before *Glory* left harbour. Once at sea the carrier set course for Malta again, where she

..a wrecked Sea Fury is ditched over the port side.

"Lined-up-left". A Sea Fury has "floated" over most of the arrester wires and appears to be a candidate for a barrier prang.

arrived on 9 July to prepare for the start of the Mediterranean Fleet's first summer cruise and an official visit to Istanbul. At 1140 on Monday 21 July Vice-Admiral R. A. B. Edwards, Flag Officer, Second-in-Command, Mediterranean Fleet, hoisted his flag in *Glory*, and ten minutes later the carrier left Malta. Once at sea two new squadrons, 807 and 898, with their Sea Furies, were flown on and course was set to rendezvous with the cruiser *Cleopatra*, the Canadian aircraft carrier *Magnificent* and the destroyers *Chevron* and *Chivalrous*, for the visit to Istanbul. The squadron arrived in the Sea of Marmara during the early hours of 24 July, and at 1034 that forenoon they anchored in the Bosphorus to begin what was scheduled to be a six-day visit, with departure set for 30 July.

This shot was taken just a split second before the aircraft was stopped by the barrier.

Two days before the ships had arrived in Istanbul, however, political events in Egypt were developing which would cut short the fleet's summer cruise. Egypt in 1952 was a country of deep internal contradictions, a curious blend of the archaic and the modern. The society of its cities was amongst the most cultured and sophisticated in the Middle East, but in the country areas the people were desperately poor. What united the whole population, however, was the deep resentment at Britain's retention of armed forces in the Suez Canal Zone, which was regarded as a colonial presence in an independent country. Violence followed and from January 1952 there was a guerrilla war between troops in the Canal Zone and Egyptian nationalists. Meanwhile, a group of Egyptian Army officers led by the fiercely patriotic Colonel Gamal Abdul Nassar and Anwar-el-Sadat were plotting to take over the country's government. They were known to be against any British military presence in Egypt. Their main political concern, however, was the corrupt administration of King Farouk, who had succeeded his father Fuad in 1936. Farouk had made a habit of appointing his own favourites as government ministers. It was his stubborn refusal to dismiss such ministers - even after it had been proved that they were conducting arms deals and buying defective weapons at vast profits to themselves. The matter came to a head in July 1952 when Farouk made known his intention of appointing his own brother-in-law as War Minister, which led to a coup by the Army officers. They acted during the evening of 22 July, and by the morning of 26 July Army tanks had surrounded Farouk's Ras-al-Tin Palace in the city of Alexandria. That same day Farouk abdicated and sailed for Naples in his luxury yacht Mahroussa. With only two killed and seven wounded the coup had been virtually bloodless, and for the time being General Naguib became Head of State, although Nassar and Sadat held the real reins of power. Both men were convinced that a British Army would invade Egypt. In fact Farouk had asked that British troops occupy Cairo and, if necessary, Alexandria. However, the Prime Minister, Winston Churchill, wisely demurred, but in case of widespread civil unrest in the country the Government ordered naval units to move closer to Egypt.

While *Glory* and the other ships lay at Istanbul, the evening of 26 July, saw a sudden recall of liberty men. Steam was ordered to be raised immediately. In the event the squadron, including *Glory*, left Istanbul at 0400 on Sunday 27 July, bound for North Africa and the coast of Libya. At the same time other units of the Mediterranean Fleet, including the cruisers *Birmingham* and *Glasgow*, the fast minelayer *Manxman*, the frigates *Cygnet*, *Magpie* and *Mermaid*, and the tank landing craft *Dieppe*, with 600 men of the 1st Battalion Highland Light Infantry onboard, all left Malta for North Africa. The official communique described their mission as being, "In connexion with the safeguarding of British interests in Egypt, should the necessity arise." After a fast passage south, *Glory*, arrived in Tobruk's outer harbour during the afternoon of 28 July, where Admiral Edwards transferred to *Glasgow*. By then it was becoming clear that there was no immediate threat to British interests in Egypt and that, in the short term at least, Britain's relations with Egypt had actually improved. That same evening the force was ordered to Cyprus, and during the evening of 30 July *Glory* anchored off Larnaca, where shore leave was granted to the off-duty watch. The carrier remained at Larnaca for six days, during which time she was opened for visits from the British service personnel serving nearby. On Tuesday 5 August she weighed anchor and put to sea for four days of flying practice, but after four more days off Larnaca, with the diplomatic crisis in Egypt having eased, *Glory* and the other units of the fleet weighed anchor and set course for Malta. On 15 August, having flown off the squadrons to Hal Far, the carrier entered Grand Harbour.

Glory remained at Malta until Monday 1 September, when she left harbour to land on the nine Sea Furies of 801 Squadron and the eight Fireflies of 821 Squadron, which were to be her new Air Group. For ten days the carrier carried out an intensive period of flying training off Malta, with a break over the weekend of 5 September. During this period there was only one major mishap when, at 0737 on 10 September, Sea Fury 162 was lost over the side on launching. Fortunately, the pilot was rescued by the destroyer *Chieftain*. Two days later *Glory* returned to Grand Harbour to prepare for her next official visit. This time, flying the flag of Vice-Admiral F. R. Parham, Flag Officer (Flotillas) Mediterranean, and accompanied by the destroyers *Chequers*, *Chevron* and *Chieftain*, she was to pay a five-day visit to Spain's second city, Barcelona. The force left Malta at 1130

On 23 May 1952 *Glory* passed through the Suez Canal to serve with the Mediterranean Fleet for just over five months. It was a break from operations off Korea. As *Glory* passed the British military base on the Suez Canal Zone the band of the 1st Battalion Coldstream Guards greeted her.

on 12 September and after a passage of three days made a ceremonial entry into the Spanish port where they secured alongside. Diplomatically, the visit to Barcelona was extremely important for it was the first time since before the start of the Spanish Civil War that Royal Navy ships had visited the port, with the last visit to Barcelona being in 1933. At a diplomatic level there were receptions in honour of senior Spanish Government ministers, while the ships' companies were treated to a programme of entertainment arranged by the city authorities. For three days the ships were opened to the public and, needless to say,

Glory proved to be very popular. The visit ended on Saturday 20 September, when the fleet sailed for Malta again, with flying practice being carried out en route.

On her return *Glory* completed a seven-day maintenance period, before undergoing another five days of flying training in the exercise areas off Malta. On 3 October she returned to Grand Harbour, but six days later, on Thursday 9 October, in company with the destroyer *Daring*, she left Malta bound once more for the Far East - and operations off Korea.

Chapter Eight

Home At Last
October 1952 - July 1953

When *Glory* and *Daring* left Malta during the afternoon of 9 October 1952, they were seen off by aircraft from both RNAS Hal Far and RAF Luqa, which flew past in formation. They were also followed by four units of the 1st Destroyer Squadron, led by Captain (D) in *Chequers*, which steamed past *Glory* with farewell signals flying. On passage, flying practice included carrier controlled approaches and tactical reconnaissance flights of up to 60 miles inland over Libya. At 1730 on 12 October both ships arrived at Port Said. Before the Suez Canal transit one of the carrier's midshipmen was disembarked to the British Army hospital ashore for an appendectomy, from which he made a full recovery. Between 0400 and 1600 on 13 October both *Glory* and *Daring* made a direct canal transit, and in the northern area of the Red Sea flying practice was resumed, with particular attention being paid to weapon training. At 1200 on 15 October *Daring* was detached to make an informal three-day visit to Port Sudan, after which she returned to Suez. Meanwhile, *Glory* arrived in Aden early on 17 October, sailing 24 hours later with *INS Rana* (formerly *HMS Raider*) in company. She also had three Indian naval pilots and three aircraft artificers on board for the passage to Singapore. They showed great interest in all the ship's activities, and were able to witness all the flying operations. As she left Aden the carrier passed the cruiser *Belfast*, which was on her way home to pay off after a three-year commission in the Far East. On 18 October the aircraft from both 801 and 821 Squadrons carried out a dummy strike on Aden, and as the ship steamed across the Arabian Sea they carried out a navigational exercise over India's south-western province of Travancore.

As *Glory* steamed south of Ceylon the cruiser *Kenya* should have been carrying out air and surface exercises with her, but with Mau Mau violence having erupted in Kenya and a state of emergency having been declared the cruiser had been ordered to Mombasa. On 23 October, *Rana* was detached to col-

lect mail, and *Glory's* aircraft practised reconnaissance flights over southern Ceylon. On Monday 27 October, when *Glory* was steaming south through the Strait of Malacca, her aircraft flew 30 sorties to attack a Malayan terrorist gang who were hiding in the Kuala Langat forest reserve in south-western Selangor. The attacks were co-ordinated with a troop of No 93 Field Battery, Royal Artillery, who also shelled the terrorists.

Glory arrived in Singapore on 28 October, and three days later was bound for Hong Kong. Once off the coast of Hong Kong the carrier remained at sea for two days to take part in "Exercise Taipan", to test the naval and air defence capabilities of the colony. The Commander of British Forces, Hong Kong, General Sir Terence Airey, was flown on board and remained in the ship to observe the exercises. At 0827 on Monday 3 November, a Firefly, flown by Lieutenant B. V. Bacon, and carrying a rating as a passenger, ditched on take-off. Fortunately, they were both rescued safely by the destroyer *Comus*. They rejoined the ship two hours later.

At 0430 on Tuesday 4 November *Glory* rendezvoused with her sister *Ocean*, which had left Sasebo three days earlier, and both carriers exercised together. After transferring five Sea Furies, three Fireflies and two Dragonfly SAR helicopters from *Ocean* to *Glory*, both carriers then entered Hong Kong harbour later that afternoon. Once in harbour *Glory* took over from *Ocean* and at 1545 on 6 November, she left with *Comus* to carry out bombardment exercises, leaving *Ocean* to spend two more days in harbour before she left to return to Malta. As *Glory* and *Comus* steamed towards Sasebo they ran into north-easterly gales and heavy seas which, on 7 November, stopped all flying. On board the destroyer a large crack was found in the hull plating and she was detached to steam on ahead for urgent repairs. On the next day, with the weather having moderated, the aircraft were able to carry out divisional drill and radio calibration exercises. By the time *Glory* arrived in

Sasebo at 0930 on Sunday 9 November, Captain Maunsell was able to report: "801 Sea Fury Squadron and 821 Firefly Squadron are now fully worked up and the ship is ready to start her third tour of duty with the United Nations Forces."

At 0700 on Monday 10 November, flying the flag of FO2 FES, Rear-Admiral E. G. A. Clifford, *Glory* left Sasebo for her first patrol off the west coast of Korea. During the initial three days it had been intended that the squadrons would carry out as much reconnaissance as possible over the operational area in order to familiarize aircrews with the area and to provide up-to-date target information. On 11 November, however, the first operational day, bad weather made it necessary to postpone flying until the afternoon and even then low cloud, rain and poor visibility over the target area made attacks and reconnaissance difficult. During the second, third and fourth days strong north-easterly winds, which reached gale force at times, again made for difficult flying conditions. All the aircraft were engaged in attacks on coastal guns, and they also carried out spotting duties for the cruiser *Birmingham*, which was bombarding coastal gun positions on the mainland adjacent to Yonpyon-do. Troops and gun positions in the coastal area of the mainland near Ch-do were also attacked by the aircraft. Armed reconnaissance missions of coastal areas round the island of Sosuap-to were carried out on three successive days, in order to detect any build-up of troops or landing craft which might have indicated an invasion of the friendly islands in that area. In addition systematic attacks were carried out on railway and road bridges, as well as railway tunnels, rolling stock and convoys of ox-carts, which were being used to carry ammunition. Apart from the first sortie on the first day and on each of the last two days, the Sea Furies carried two 500lb bombs; during the armed reconnaissance missions they were armed with 20mm ammunition only. The Fireflies carried eight rockets fitted with 60lb high explosive warheads, except on the last day when 12 sorties were flown with four rockets per aircraft and 11 with two 1,000lb bombs per aircraft. The armed reconnaissance missions, with no bombs and only four rockets, were necessary in order to remain within the ship's allowance of explosive stores.

On 13 November came the first fatality when a Sea Fury being flown by Lieutenant R. Newell-Jones was hit by anti-aircraft fire whilst the pilot was leading his division in a dive-bombing attack on a railway bridge south of Sariwon. The aircraft crashed in marshy ground, with the loss of the pilot. That same day a Firefly being flown by Lieutenant (E) D. F. Robbins, was hit by flak and suffered a loss of coolant. Fortunately the pilot was able to ditch his aircraft in the sea off the island of Paengyong-do and was rescued by a helicopter from the US base on the island. During the patrol nine Sea Furies and six Fireflies were damaged by enemy fire, with another of the latter being damaged by its own ammunition exploding in the gun. The patrol ended at Sasebo on Thursday 20 November. Six days later FO2 transferred his flag to *Unicorn*, which had arrived from Singapore with aircraft from *Ocean*, of which two Fireflies were allocated to *Glory*.

When *Glory* left Sasebo at 0700 on Friday 28 November, Captain Maunsell was suffering from a severe attack of gastritis so the ship was taken to sea by the Executive Officer, Cdr D. E. Bromley-Martin. Although Captain Maunsell returned to duty the next day, on 30 November he was taken ill again and transferred to *Consort* for passage to Sasebo. In the meantime, Cdr Bromley-Martin was appointed Acting Captain and took command of *Glory*. During this second patrol flying had to be cancelled on three days, and flying operations which were planned for the afternoon of replenishment day were curtailed because of bad weather. Nine aircraft which had been launched had to return to the ship without attacking their targets. During the patrol, systematic attacks were made on rail and road bridges, transport and troop concentrations, while close air support was also provided for Commonwealth troops - although bad weather prevented a second such mission. During the patrol ten aircraft were damaged by flak, and one plane was forced to ditch. This incident occurred on Saturday 6 December when, after attacking a troop concentration south-west of Haeju, a Firefly being flown by Lieutenant J. G. Marshall was hit by small arms fire which caused a coolant leak. The pilot managed to ditch his aircraft in the sea, some 26 miles from the ship, but within 20 minutes he was rescued by the ship's helicopter. *Glory's* second patrol ended at Kure during the afternoon of Tuesday 9 December.

On Sunday 14 December, whilst the carrier was at Kure, Captain E. D. G. Lewin DSO DSC* RN,

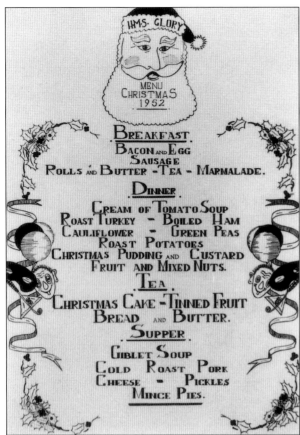

IHMS·GLORY

MENU
CHRISTMAS
1952

BREAKFAST
BACON AND EGG
SAUSAGE
ROLLS AND BUTTER - TEA - MARMALADE.

DINNER
CREAM OF TOMATO SOUP
ROAST TURKEY - BOILED HAM
CAULIFLOWER - GREEN PEAS
ROAST POTATOES
CHRISTMAS PUDDING AND CUSTARD
FRUIT AND MIXED NUTS.

TEA
CHRISTMAS CAKE - TINNED FRUIT
BREAD AND BUTTER.

SUPPER
GIBLET SOUP
COLD ROAST PORK
CHEESE - PICKLES
MINCE PIES.

Glory's 1952 Christmas Day menu. With Christmas having been spent at sea off Korea, the ship's company had a belated celebration on New Year's Eve.

relieved A/Captain Bromley-Martin, who resumed his duties as Executive Officer. Captain Lewin was a distinguished Fleet Air Arm Officer, who had flown the Sea Fox from *Ajax* during the Battle of the River Plate for which he was awarded the DSC.

Glory left Kure for her third patrol at 0800 on Monday 15 December, and with better weather than her previous patrols, flying was only restricted during one forenoon. Once again the aircraft targeted road and rail transport, troop concentrations and stores depots, with the Sea Furies directing their main effort at railway bridges. In the latter half of the patrol an unusual amount of rolling stock was discovered, which provided lucrative targets. For two days just prior to Christmas the squadrons provided close air support for troops of the Commonwealth Division, who were under attack by massed waves of Chinese troops. Sadly there were a number of casualties dur-

ing this period, the first on Tuesday 16 December when one of the SAR Dragonfly helicopters, having been caught by a strong crosswind, crashed into the sea, with the loss of its two crew members, Lieutenant A. P. Daniels and Aircrewman 1 E. R. Ripley. The second came during the afternoon of Saturday 20 December, when Firefly 205, flown by Lieutenant P. G. Fogden, crashed into the sea following an explosion in its wing. There was no sign of the aircraft or the pilot, and the cause would appear to have been 20mm cannon ammunition exploding in the gun. This, being the second such incident, led to a full-scale investigation into the problem.

Glory spent Christmas Day at sea, with flying operations beginning at 0845 and continuing until 1730. It was on Christmas Day that the fourth casualty occured when, during an attack on a railway bridge west of Haeju, the Firefly being flown by Lieutenant R. E. Barrett, was shot down. The aircraft was seen to be spinning out of control at 1,000 feet and on impact with the ground it exploded in a ball of flame.

The final day of flying operations took place on 27 December, and next day *Glory* steamed off towards the Iwakuni air base so that four replacement Fireflies could be flown on. Finally, at 0730 on Monday 29 December *Glory* secured to her buoy at Sasebo where the New Year could be celebrated.

At 0700 on Sunday 4 January 1953 *Glory* once again sailed from Sasebo to begin her fourth patrol, but once again bad weather badly disrupted the flying programme. The atrocious weather conditions caused the cancellation of what was the equivalent of two full days' flying, with no operational flying at all on 9 January. Two days earlier flying had not started until 1230, and the transfer of ammunition from the cruiser *Newcastle* had taken place in a snowstorm with 27 knot winds. With railway bridges being repaired quickly after each raid, it was decided that during this patrol railway cuttings would be targeted. Although weather conditions made railway reconnaissance difficult, 33 railway cuttings were attacked on the lines from Changyon and Haeju to Pyongyang. However, it soon became clear that most of this bomb damage had been repaired within 48 hours. Troops and supply dumps were attacked and spotting missions were flown for the battleship *USS Missouri* in the Cho-do area, and for the frigate *Sparrow* which carried out a bombardment south of Haeju.

On 5 January flying operations began at dawn, and that day Sea Fury VX 640 suffered a complete electrical failure whilst airborne, but Sub-Lieutenant G. B. S. Foster managed to make a successful wheels-up landing at Paengyong-do. Later that morning Lieutenant (E) D. G. Mather was shot down in the Chaeryong area but, despite being shot at from the ground, he bailed out successfully and parachuted to the ground where he was captured by Communist troops. He subsequently spent eight harrowing months in captivity, before being repatriated in September 1953. Not knowing what fate had befallen Lieutenant Mather, a rescue helicopter was summoned from Cho-do, but one of its escorting aircraft, Sea Fury WE 689, from *Glory*, crashed while on the mission with the loss of the pilot, Sub-Lieutenant B. E. Raynor. Early that afternoon, because of low cloud, flying was suspended for just over an hour. When it resumed there was another fatality. At 16.30, Sub-Lieutenant J. M. Simmonds' Firefly, WF 622, was seen to crash with the loss of the pilot. The day's flying operations had taken a heavy toll in young lives.

Next day, 6 January, flying started early. That afternoon FO2, Rear-Admiral Clifford, arrived on board by helicopter from *Birmingham*, and a few minutes later the Commander of the US 7th Fleet, Vice-Admiral J. J. Clark USN, and the Commander Task Force 95, Rear-Admiral J. E. Ginnrich USN, arrived on board by helicopter from *USS Missouri*. Both men remained on board until completion of flying operations that day, when they left in their respective helicopters. The versatility of the helicopter for all manner of duties was becoming apparent. At 1630 that day, Firefly VT 412, being flown by Lieutenant W. R. Heaton, was forced to ditch in the sea north of the island of Kirin-do, after being hit by small arms fire. After successfully ditching his aircraft and taking to his life-raft, Lieutenant Heaton was rescued by an American helicopter and returned to the ship at 1720, where he was greeted by the visiting VIPs; the helicopter crew were rewarded with a bottle of Scotch whisky. That same day saw 821 Squadron's 1,000th deck landing since joining *Glory* four months earlier.

Sunday 11 January saw the final day of operations, with flying beginning at dawn, and although a number of aircraft suffered damage, there were no further casualties. At just after midnight on Tuesday 13 January *Glory* anchored off Kure, where it had been intended that she would enter the port's dry dock. A survey of the dock, however, had found that it was unfit to accommodate a vessel of *Glory's* size and so, at 1130 she moored to a buoy in the harbour for her six-day break. With large quantities of stores and equipment to embark, together with a busy mainte-

On 6 January 1953, Vice-Admiral J. J. Clark USN, commander of the US 7th Fleet, visited *Glory*. Here he arrives in a US Navy helicopter.

Sea Furies from *Glory* flying over a frozen sea during the winter of 1953. The carrier's escort ships were required to act as icebreakers in order to prevent ice floes interfering with flying operations.

nance schedule to complete, the short breaks at Sasebo and Kure were hardly rest periods for the ship's company. There was time, however, for some sightseeing and the local canteen and bars were well frequented. There were also opportunities for some sport, and the departmental soccer teams were able to organize a tournament, which was won by the Royal Marines Detachment.

On Monday 19 January *Glory* sailed from Kure to relieve *USS Badoeng Strait* on Korea's west coast, and to begin her fifth patrol. By now the hard Korean winter weather had set in, and the sheltered waters around the friendly islands were virtually icebound. In order to prevent the ice floes interfering with flying operations the escort ships were required to act as ice breakers so that the UN task force could continue to

Lieutenant V. B. Mitchell's Sea Fury with its record of rocket and bombing sorties flown.

use the area. With the islands in renewed danger of invasion *Glory's* aircraft attacked enemy troop concentrations and guns in coastal areas of the mainland. Fortunately, only one aircraft was damaged, a Firefly flown by Commissioned Pilot M. Kent, which suffered a fault with its landing hook after which he was ordered to make a landing at Paengyong-do. Having landed in about a foot of water the plane tipped onto its nose, but the pilot was not injured and the plane was later recovered. *Glory's* involvement in the patrol ended at 1245 on Thursday 29 January, when she secured to No 19 buoy in Sasebo Harbour.

Glory's sixth patrol began at 0730 on Thursday 5 February when, in company with the destroyers *Charity* and *Consort*, she left Sasebo to set course for the operational area. Because intelligence reports indicated that hostile submarines might be operating in the area, Captain Lewin decided to fly an anti-submarine screen of one Firefly during daylight hours. Combined with the fact that submarines were suspected in the area, the shallow waters of the region and the fact that the escorts lacked recent anti-submarine training resulted in a number of spurious contacts. In each case emergency turns were made and on one occasion the escorting destroyer dropped depth charges. Flying operations began on 6 February, with the main air effort being directed against troop concentrations and stores dumps. Special attention was given to villages 12 miles south-west of Chinnampo, which were reported to be housing about 1,400 enemy troops whose mission, according to intelligence reports, was to be "partisan subjugation". Attacks were also made on villages 11 miles west of Ongjin, in which enemy troops were reported to be massing with boats for attacks on friendly islands. Two missions a day were also devoted to attacking the rail system. On 8 and 14 February pre-dawn strikes were launched at 0520 in the hope of catching transport on the roads, and a large number of trucks were attacked in the Chinnampo-Marchon-Pyongyang triangle. On 14 February a total of 75 sorties were flown, which was the greatest number achieved on one day since the carrier returned to Korean waters in November 1952.

On 6 February a flight of four Sea Furies was attacked by two enemy MiG-15s, but fortunately no damage was caused. On the morning of 8 February, whilst attacking road transport, Sea Fury WJ 286 suffered high oil temperature and low pressure, but the pilot, Sub-Lieutenant J. F. Belville, made a successful landing at Paengyong-do. On 9 February Sub-Lieutenant M. Hayes, who was flying on only his third sortie, in Sea Fury WH 582, was hit by flak and the aircraft's oil system was damaged. Fortunately, he was able to ditch in the sea and was quickly rescued by a US helicopter and transferred to the destroyer *Anzac*. That same day Firefly WB 366, flown by Sub-Lieutenant P. Millett, and carrying an Army passenger, Captain R. Bury RA, ditched in the sea. As he was landing on, and after he had been given the "Cut", the plane's wing drooped away and the aircraft started to swing to starboard. Despite the pilot's efforts to keep the aircraft straight, it plunged over the starboard side into the Yellow Sea. Even though the aircraft was upside down, below the surface and with Captain Bury badly injured, both men managed to extricate themselves and were rescued by *Comus*. Captain Bury subsequently spent 18 months in hospital and was invalided out of the Army. Next day, immediately after launch, Lieutenant Dallosso's Firefly, VX 431, suffered engine trouble and he was forced to jettison his depth charges before attempting to land back on. Before he had completed his circuit, however, the engine cut out and he ditched in the sea four miles off *Glory's* port bow. Fortunately, both he and his observer, Sub-Lieutenant Harrison, were rescued without delay by the destroyer *USS Hanna*. At 1310 on 11 February, Lieutenant C. A. MacPherson, whose Sea Fury had been damaged by anti-aircraft fire on two previous occasions, was hit by flak. He was killed when his plane crashed on a hillside and burst into flames. The final fatality of the patrol came at the close of flying on Saturday 14 February, when a flight of five Sea Furies and five Fireflies were landing on. Unfortunately, Sea Fury WJ 239, flown by Sub-Lieutenant R. D. Bradley, suffered an engine failure and crashed into the sea on the starboard side of the ship. Although the pilot had managed to jettison his hood, the aircraft hit the water at a speed of at least 140 knots, and it broke up on impact and sank. Sadly there was no trace of Sub-Lieutenant Bradley. On completion of the final day of flying operations on Sunday 15 February, *Glory* left the operational area and at 0715 on Tuesday 17 February, with the assistance of "Operation Pinwheel", the carrier secured alongside at Kure.

The end of a patrol. On 24 February 1953, *Glory* arrives alongside at Kure, aided by "Operation Pinwheel". This required the piston engined aircraft to be firmly lashed to the flightdeck, both forward and aft. By running up their engines and co-ordinating their output, the aircraft could help turn the ship or push her onto the berth.

After only seven days in harbour, during the forenoon of Tuesday 24 February, *Glory* shifted to an anchorage in the outer harbour before sailing at 1730 that day for her seventh patrol. Despite the fact that during this patrol *Glory* experienced the worst weather since her return to the Far East, with fog, rain, snow and gale force winds, the main air effort was again directed against troop concentrations and stores dumps. Since the start of her operations in Korean waters great efforts had been made to build up a close liaison with guerrilla groups operating ashore, and in particular with the First Partisan Infantry Regiment. As a result a great deal of information regarding targets was received on board. This liaison benefited both *Glory* and the partisans, and during the patrol two signals from the latter were received on board giving the results of air strikes which had been carried out. On Monday 2 March, a group of partisans signalled from the island of Pae-som that they were under attack from a force of 40 enemy troops. Despite the fact that bad weather meant only defensive sorties were being flown, two Sea Fury pilots who were being briefed for CAP duties were ordered to carry out an urgent strike in support of the partisans. In the event the two planes were flown by Lt-Cdr P. B. Stuart, the CO of 801 Squadron, and Lt E. R. Anson, attacked the enemy troops and inflicted severe casualties - to the relief of the partisans who later signalled

their thanks to the ship. At 0500 on Thursday 5 March, in what was to be a pre-dawn strike, two Sea Furies had been launched when the ship again ran into thick fog and the rest of the launch had to be cancelled. As a result Captain Lewin reluctantly decided that he would not risk any more pre-dawn missions until the foggy season was over. With the last sorties being launched during the afternoon of Friday 6 March, the carrier arrived at Sasebo during the following afternoon for an eight-day break.

Glory's eighth patrol began at 0630 on Sunday 15 March when, in company with the destroyers *Charity*, *Athabaskan* and *USS Cowell*, she left Sasebo. Flying operations began next day and with the spring thaw having started, attacks were made on rail and road bridges, tunnels and road transport. During the patrol only one Sea Fury made an emergency landing at Paengyong-do. Both the plane and the pilot returned safely to the ship. On 24 March poor visibility disrupted flying and, with no improvement the next day, the carrier made her way to Kure where she berthed on 27 March, adjacent to the maintenance carrier *Unicorn* which had brought aircraft replacements from Singapore.

On 25 March Her Majesty Queen Mary, the widow of King George V, died and six days later, on Tuesday 31 March, her funeral took place. As a mark of respect, at 1110 that day the combined ships' compa-

Life on one of *Glory's* mess decks in the early 1950s. It appears that dinner has just been served. In those days the men lived, ate and slept on the mess decks.

nies of *Glory* and *Unicorn* cleared lower deck and held a memorial service on the jetty.

At 1800 on Thursday 2 April *Glory* left Kure once again, to begin her ninth period of operations two days later. As ever the main enemy targets were bridges, tunnels, troop concentrations and stores dumps. Again fog hampered flying operations, but on Sunday 5 April Captain Lewin put into practice a theory that a carrier equipped with 33 aircraft should be capable of launching 12 sorties every daylight hour. In the event this was surpassed, with 123 sorties being launched in eight hours, which equalled a record set by *Ocean* in the summer of 1952. During the day, flight deck and maintenance crews had to work industriously to keep up serviceability throughout. This included changing the complete tailplane of one machine. As for the aircrews, there was even more pressure, with all pilots flying at least four sorties, and some five, during the day. With only two aircraft having been damaged by enemy action, the patrol ended at 1815 on Sunday 12 April, when *Glory* secured once again to No 18 buoy in Sasebo Harbour. Having had only a six-day break, at 1830 on Saturday 18 April, the carrier

The signal sent by *Glory* on 5 April 1953 to the C-in-C Far East Station, and to the Admiralty as a Press Release, when she equalled the record number of sorties which had been set by *Ocean* the previous year.

sailed for her tenth patrol. Before leaving the area, however, new pilots were given the opportunity to carry out some deck landing practice, and fresh aircraft were flown on from Iwakuni. With an exchange of prisoners of war taking place *Glory's* target areas were more limited than usual, but once again her pilots prevented enemy troop movements down the west coast, and along the rail and road arteries inland, destroying coastal guns, providing close air support for the troops ashore and attacking concentrations of enemy reinforcements. On 23 April four Sea Furies on a reconnaissance run were attacked by two MiG-15s, but fortunately damage was limited to just one hit. At 1704 on Saturday 25 April, Lieutenant J. T.

```
FLYING PROGRAMME-RECORD BREAKER FOR SUNDAY 5th APRIL
        Duty Officers 801 Bawden 821 Lt. Agnew
```

Event	Off	On	A/C	Mission	C/S	Crews
A	0645	0805	2 Fu	C.A.P.	54	BLUE GREG
			4 Fu	Strike	52	PEAR PSON KETE BYES
			3 Fu	Strike	53	LEAH FIDO MICH
			6 Fi	Strike	77	SAMP BANN SKIN ROBB KENT SHER
B	0805	0925	2 Fu	C.A.P.	88	BAKE BAWD
			4 Fu	Strike	51	C.O. BELL SMIT ANSN
			3 Fu	Strike	55	HAND FOST CRAW
			6 Fi	Strike	76	C.O./WEST MILL GARV HAMN MARS GRAI
C	0925	1045	2 Fu	C.A.P.	99	AIR KETE
			4 Fu	Strike	52	PEAR PSON BLUE HYES
			4 Fu	Strike	53	LEAH GREG FIDO MICH
			6 Fi	Strike	77	SMAP BERR SKIN ROBB KENT SHER
D	1045	1205	2 Fu	C.A.P.	88	LAYO BELL
			3 Fu	A.R.	51	C.O. SMIT ANSN
			4 Fu	Strike	55	HAND BAWD FOST CRAW
			6 Fi	Strike	76	C.O./HARI MILL GARV HAMN MARS GRAI
E	1205	1325	2 Fu	C.A.P.	99	AIR PSON
			4 Fu	Strike	52	PEAR KETE BLUE HYES
			4 Fu	Strike	53	LEAH GREG FIDO MICH
			4 Fi	Strike	77	SAMP BANN SKIN ROBB
			2 Fi	Tarcap	80	KENT SHER
F	1325	1445	2 Fu	C.A.P.	88	BAKE FOST
			4 Fu	Tarcap	51	C.O. BELL SMIT ANSN
			3 Fu	A.R.	55	HAND BAWD CRAW
			2 Fi	Tarcap	76	C.O. MILL
			4 Fi	Strike	79	GARV/COLE HAMN MARS GRAI
G	1445	1605	2 Fu	C.A.P.	52	PEAR MICH
			3 Fu	Strike	53	LEAH PSON FIDO
			4 Fu	Strike	54	BLUE HYES KETE GREG
			4 Fi	Strike	77	SAMP BANN KENT BERR
			2 Fi	Tarcap	80	SKIN ROBB
H	1605	1705	2 Fu	C.A.P.	88	LAYO ANSN
			4 Fi	Tarcap	76	C.O. MILL GARV HAMN
J	1705	1815	2 Fu	C.A.P.	53	LEAH HYES
			4 Fi	Tarcap	78	MARS/AGNE BANN GRAI SHER
K	1845	1925	2 Fu	C.A.P.	51	C.O. SMIT
			2 Fu	Tarcap	55	HAND FOST

Flying Stations:- 0545 Cat Required:- 0645 Briefing:- 20 mins before launch

ORDNANCE:- Fury 2 x 500 except on A.R. and C.A.P.
           Firefly 8 x 60 lb R/P throughout.
           Bombs Required:- 104 x 500lb. R/P Required:- 384 x 60lb.

FUEL:- Fury full internal plus full drop-tanks.
       Firefly full internal plus half nacelles.

NOTES:- 1. No C.A.S. - Gun co-ordination or Courier.
        2. Helicopter required after event ABLE.

WHEELS UP:- Peangyong Do 0945 - 1245
            Chodo   0945 - 1545

```
Moon Rise          0107
Nautical Twilight  0625
Sunrise            0723
Sunset             2009
Nautical Twilight  2106
```

(See)

Glory's flying programme for 5 April 1953.

McGregor's Sea Fury, which was taking part in a strike on bridges south of Sariwon, was hit by anti-aircraft fire and crashed in flames, with the loss of the pilot. No less than an hour and a half later, at 1835, Sub-Lieutenant W. J. B. Keates was shot down while bombing ammunition stores close to Changyon. Sadly, he was another fatality. The patrol ended at 1045 on Wednesday 29 April, when *Glory* secured alongside at Kure.

Glory's final patrol off Korea began at 1150 on Monday 4 May, and next day she arrived in the operational area. During the patrol flying was again much restricted by poor visibility, and even on the two fine days the visibility was not good. This was attributed to minute particles of sand suspended in the atmosphere which had blown from the Gobi Desert by strong north-westerly winds. These poor weather conditions caused the cancellation of 135 sorties. Once again the targets were mainly troops, bridges and

A Firefly about to catch a wire as it touches down.

This Firefly has actually taken a wire. Note the bowsprings holding up the wires above the deck, which made it easier for the hook to catch.

As a Sea Fury lands on a naval airman runs towards the aircraft and, once it has stopped, he will disengage the arrester wire from the hook.

The officers and men of *Glory's* Dragonfly helicopter flight.

Personnel of the Flight Deck Department pose for an informal photograph.

At 1439 on Thursday 14 May 1953, the last aircraft flown on operations over Korea landed on, and...

stores, but some attacks were made on coastal guns. A radar station, whose position had been reported by partisans, was destroyed. At 0930 on 8 May, while strafing enemy troops on the Ongjin Peninsular, Lieutenant W. R. Sherlock's Firefly was hit by small arms fire and the pilot was forced to ditch in the sea. Fortunately he was rescued by the frigate *St Bride's Bay*. *Glory's* last sorties were flown between 0645 and 1330 on Thursday 14 May, and although targets were considered "safe", some anti-aircraft fire was encountered. Four Sea Furies, flown by Lieutenants Anson and Mitchell and Sub-Lieutenants Hayes and Pearson, flew on a mission to provide air support for partisans ashore. On completion they flew direct to Iwakuni, Japan. With the last aircraft, a Firefly flown by Lieutenant B. V. Bacon, having landed on at 1439, *Glory* set course for Iwakuni herself. That evening, at 1800, the lower deck was cleared and a memorial service was held on the flight deck to commemorate all the officers and men who had lost their lives during the carrier's latest tour of duty off Korea - a considerable number of young men.

...the pilot, Lieutenant B. V. Bacon, is welcomed back on board.

100

ROLL OF HONOUR

~1951~

LIEUTENANT (P) EDWARD PETER LANGDALE STEPHENSON.	28 APRIL
PILOT (3) STANLEY WILLIAM EDWIN FORD.	5 JUNE
LIEUTENANT (P) JOHN HARRY SHARP.	28 JUNE
AIRCREWMAN (1) GEORGE BERTRAM WELLS.	28 JUNE
LIEUTENANT (P) ROBERT WILLIAMS.	16 JULY
SUB LIEUTENANT (O) IAN ROBERTSON SHEPLEY.	16 JULY
COMMISSIONED PILOT TERENCE WILLIAM SPARKE.	18 JULY
SUB LIEUTENANT (O) RONALD GEORGE ALBERT DAVEY.	22 SEPT

~1952~

LIEUTENANT (P) RICHARD JAMES OVERTON.	15 MAR
LIEUTENANT (P) RICHARD NEVILL-JONES.	18 NOV
PETTY OFFICER (AIR) VICTOR COLMAN.	19 NOV

~1952~

LIEUTENANT (P) ALAN PHILIP DANIELS.	16 DEC
AIRCREWMAN (1) ERNEST RAYMOND RIPLEY.	16 DEC
LIEUTENANT (P) PETER GEORGE FOGDEN.	20 DEC
LIEUTENANT (P) ROBERT EDWARD BARRETT.	25 DEC

~1953~

SUB LIEUTENANT (P) BRIAN EDWARD RAYNER.	5 JAN
SUB LIEUTENANT (P) JAMES MALCOLM SIMONDS.	5 JAN
LIEUTENANT (P) CEDRIC ALEXANDER MACPHERSON.	10 FEB
SUB LIEUTENANT (P) RICHARD DEREK BRADLEY.	14 FEB
LIEUTENANT (P) JOHN THOMAS McGREGOR.	25 APR
SUB LIEUTENANT (P) WALTER JOHN BUTLER KEATES.	25 APR

"LEST WE FORGET"

Before *Glory* left Korean waters a memorial service was held on the flight deck. This roll of honour is a permanent memorial to those who were killed in action during operations in Korea. This memorial is now displayed at the Fleet Air Arm Museum, Yeovilton.

On Friday 15 May, with the ship off Iwakuni, five Fireflies and three Sea Furies were flown off to the air base for transfer to *Ocean*, which was replacing *Glory* in Korean waters. At 2030 she anchored off the coast. Next day, at 1020, *Glory* weighed anchor and at 0710 on Sunday 17 May, just 20 minutes after *Ocean* had arrived in the port from Hong Kong, *Glory* secured to No 19 buoy in Sasebo Harbour. During the next 48 hours stores, personnel and equipment were transferred to *Ocean* and a number of congratulatory signals were received on board. One of these, from Vice-Admiral Clark USN read: "Well done to the officers and men *HMS Glory* on completion of an outstanding tour of duty in Korean waters. You have been a valuable member of the United Nations team." Another from FO2 FES read: "My congratulations to all of you

on the satisfactory completion of your strenuous and valuable tour of operations off the west coast of Korea. You may well look back with great pride on your achievements in this war to which you have contributed so much towards defeating enemy aggression and upholding the prestige of the Royal Navy. I look forward to coming on board to thank you personally and say goodbye before you sail."

Glory had completed the longest period of air operations by any Commonwealth carrier during the Korean campaign. Since leaving the UK in January 1951, the ship had spent 530 days at sea and steamed 157,000 miles. During that period she had completed 15 months' war service and spent 316 days at sea in Korean waters. Of a total of 13,700 flights from her deck over 9,500 had been operational sorties over

End of the Korean War - *Glory* left Sasebo for Hong Kong on 19 May 1953, and two hours later she crossed the boundary which signalled her exit from the operational area.

With the ship's company manning the flight deck, and with a guard and band paraded, *Glory* makes a ceremonial entry into Hong Kong harbour.

northern Korea. Her aircraft had taken a constant toll of enemy troops and a wide range of military targets had been attacked. During two Korean winters, ice and snow had repeatedly been cleared from the flight deck and the aircraft while operations were sustained in some of the worst weather ever experienced by naval aircrews. *Glory's* Fireflies and Sea Furies had attacked rail and road transport by night in northern Korea, and a notable feature of daylight operations had been the close air support provided for the British Commonwealth Division in the front line.

With everyone eager to start the passage home to Portsmouth, *Glory* left Sasebo for Hong Kong on 19 May, and two hours later she crossed the boundary

"Dressed overall" in honour of *Glory*, the sampan belonging to Jenny's Side Party comes alongside the carrier.

On Thursday 25 June, proudly flying her paying-off pennant, *Glory* enters Malta's Grand Harbour during her voyage home to Portsmouth.

which signalled her exit from the operational area and the "Korea gratuity" of which her ship's company had been in receipt on pay day. She stayed in Hong Kong for five days, leaving for Singapore on 27 May. On 1 June she anchored in Singapore's Outer Roads, just off the city. After treating the residents to a magnificent firework display during the evening of 2 June, she left next day for the naval base at the north of the island. On 6 June she sailed for Aden where, 12 days later, she spent just seven hours in harbour. She made her northbound transit of the Suez Canal on 22 June. After spending four days at Malta and two days at Gibraltar, on Tuesday 7 July, after two and a half years away from home, she anchored in Falmouth Roads for Customs clearance. That evening she weighed anchor to steam up Channel and during the passage she received "Welcome Home" messages from the C-in-C Portsmouth, Admiral Sir John Edelston, and from Captain Colquhoun, who had commanded the ship during her first two operational periods off Korea. On her arrival at Spithead on the morning of 8 July naval aircraft from RNAS Ford flew past the ship in salute, and Vice-Admiral J. A. S Eccles, Flag Officer Air (Home), boarded the ship to welcome her home on behalf of the Admiralty. Finally, at 1130, after a ceremonial entry into Portsmouth Harbour, she secured alongside North Corner Jetty.

Although most members of the ship's company were able to take some leave during the 16 days alongside, it was not quite the end of the commission. During the forenoon of Friday 24 July *Glory* left Portsmouth to set course, via the Dover Strait, for Rosyth, where she arrived three days later. Soon after her arrival in Rosyth the carrier was moved into dry dock and it was not long before most members of the ship's company had received their draft chits and left the ship. A refit and another commission lay ahead.

Chapter Nine

The Final Years
August 1953 - August 1961

The summer of 1953 was spent in dry dock at Rosyth as the ship underwent her last long refit. On Thursday 3 September her new commanding officer, Captain R. T. White DSO** RN, joined the ship to relieve Captain Lewin. He left five hours later to take up an appointment as the Director of Air Warfare at the Admiralty, before going on to command *Eagle*.

On Wednesday 23 September 1953, with a new ship's company having joined the ship, *Glory* was shifted from the dry dock and secured to the basin wall at Rosyth Dockyard. Five weeks later, on Thursday 22 October, the carrier moved from the dockyard basin to a buoy in the Firth of Forth. That afternoon she left Rosyth and put to sea for engine trials. During the evening she anchored off Burntisland. Two days later she weighed anchor and set course south to anchor at Spithead during the evening of 25 October. Two days later, she steamed up harbour to make a ceremonial entrance into Portsmouth Harbour, where she secured alongside the dolphins for ammunitioning and storing to begin.

The official recommissioning ceremony took place on Saturday 31 October, and the C-in-C Portsmouth, Admiral Sir John Edelsten, visited to inspect both the ship's company at Divisions and the ship herself. Two days later *Glory* left Portsmouth Harbour to land on the Sea Furies of 801 Squadron, the Fireflies of 826 Squadron, the three Skyraider AEW1 aircraft of 849C Flight and the two Dragonfly helicopters of the ship's flight. She then steamed to Portland to begin her work-up - which would continue in the Mediterranean.

For three days the squadrons were put through their paces before the carrier left Plymouth Sound during the afternoon of 6 November, setting course for Gibraltar. Accompanying her for the passage was the destroyer *Obdurate*. After an overnight stop in Gibraltar Bay the two ships sailed for Malta. *Glory* was to take the place of *Theseus* in the Mediterranean Fleet.

She arrived in Grand Harbour during the afternoon of Friday 13 November. The commission did not get off to a good start when, during the afternoon of 17 November, a leading cook was drowned while swimming in St Paul's Bay. Next day *Glory* put to sea to continue the work-up which had started at Portland. At the end of each day she would anchor in Marsaxlokk Bay. On Saturday 21 November, with the carrier having returned to Grand Harbour for the weekend, there was another fatal accident on the flight deck when Commissioned Air Engineer F. G. Bradbrook was killed instantly by the tail rotor of a Dragonfly helicopter. The last week of November was spent at sea off Tripoli and once again the aircraft were put through their paces. At 0930 on Sunday 29 November, with the carrier having returned to Grand Harbour, the C-in-C Mediterranean Station, Admiral Lord Mountbatten, inspected the ship's company at Divisions on the flight deck. The first three weeks of December were spent mainly at sea off Malta, with a full flying schedule. On Friday 4 December, Vice-Admiral J. A. S. Eccles, Flag Officer Air (Home), and Vice-Admiral W. W. Davis, FO2 Mediterranean, flew on board to watch the day's flying operations as the carrier exercised with the cruiser *Gambia* and locally based destroyers. Finally, on 17 December, *Glory* entered Grand Harbour where Christmas and New Year were to be celebrated.

At 1330 on Monday 4 January 1954, with all the festivities over, *Glory* left Grand Harbour to begin a pattern of flying operations similar to those which had been undertaken before Christmas, with weekends being spent in Grand Harbour. On Monday 11 January, *Glory* put to sea in preparation for "Exercise Janex" with other units of the Mediterranean Fleet, including the cruisers *Bermuda* and *Glasgow* and the destroyers *Daring* and *St Kitts*. The manoeuvres took place between Malta and the coast of North Africa, but by the weekend all the units had returned to Grand

Glory at sea in November 1953, with other units of the Mediterranean Fleet.

Harbour. After undertaking a five-day maintenance period at Malta. *Glory* sailed at 0830 on Wednesday 20 January to make an official visit to the city of Naples, where she arrived 24 hours later to secure to buoys in the harbour. During the six days at Naples many members of the ship's company were able to travel to Pompeii, Capri or Rome, where some of them were granted an audience with His Holiness Pope Pius XII. Most men were loaded down after the Italian trip with gifts for home - mainly musical boxes! After leaving Naples on 27 January *Glory* returned to Malta, where she arrived two days later.

It was whilst *Glory* was in Grand Harbour during the first week of February that a number of minor acts of sabotage were discovered on board, with electrical cables being cut. Although the ship's operational capability was not affected, the damage was serious enough to warrant a full police investigation. A rating was subsequently convicted of malicious damage and sentenced to a period of imprisonment. For *Glory* herself the period in Grand Harbour ended during the forenoon of Monday 8 February, when she put to sea with the cruisers *Gambia* and *Glasgow* and the frigate *Magpie* to take part in "Exercise Febex" off Malta. The following Monday (15 February) with the carrier's Mediterranean deployment over, she left Grand Harbour to set course westwards for her passage home, via Villefranche and Gibraltar.

After leaving the French Riviera on 17 February, *Glory* exercised with the fleet carrier *Eagle*, which was on her way to Malta, and the French cruiser *Jeanne d'Arc*. Sea Hawk and Attacker jet fighters from *Eagle* made night attacks on *Glory* and her escort *Jeanne d'Arc*. On Tuesday 23 February, with *Eagle* having set course for the French base at Mers-el-Kebir, *Glory* secured alongside Gibraltar's south mole. Her stay in Gibraltar lasted for just over 36 hours before, at 0830 on Thursday 25 February 1954, she left for Portsmouth. Three days later, at 0900 on Sunday 28 February, *Glory* carried out her final fixed-wing flying operations when, as the carrier entered the Channel, she launched most of her aircraft to Lee-on-Solent. Later that forenoon she anchored in Weymouth Bay for Customs clearance. By the evening she was heading up Channel. At 0755 on Monday 1 March the two Dragonfly helicopters were flown ashore and an hour later, with her ship's company manning the flight deck, she entered harbour to

secure alongside Middle Slip Jetty. The ship's company could now take some well-earned leave, but *Glory* was to spend two weeks at a buoy in Fareham Creek. Between 9 and 13 April, large groups of Sea Cadets were embarked and *Glory* steamed out to Spithead, returning to harbour for Navy Days where she was the centre of attraction. During the three days that she was opened to the public helicopter flying displays were staged on the flight deck, and with helicopters still something of a novelty, the carrier attracted around 40,000 visitors.

In mid-May *Glory* was moved into No 14 dry dock for maintenance to her underwater hull and Rear-Admiral W. D. Couchman, Flag Officer Heavy Squadron, briefly hoisted his flag in his old ship *Glory* for five days. On Friday 28 May, two days after the departure of Admiral Couchman, Captain White relinquished his command and handed over to his Executive Officer, Cdr N. R. H. Rodney. *Glory* remained in dry dock until 2 June when she was moved back to Middle Slip Jetty. On Wednesday 7 July her new commanding officer, Captain H. W. S. Sims-Williams RN, joined the ship. By mid-August, having successfully completed her basin and inclination trials, *Glory* was moved to Pitch House Jetty where, in early September, some of her cargo, including heavy Army trucks and a car which belonged to the Chief Justice of Gibraltar, was embarked.

The ship left Portsmouth during the afternoon of Monday 13 September, to make a two-day passage to Glasgow where she secured alongside the city's King George V Dock. Once alongside she embarked five Whirlwind helicopters for 848 Squadron, nine for the RAF's 155 Squadron and two Sycamores for the RAF's 194 Squadron. With the Malayan Emergency at its height all the helicopters were destined for Singapore. Gale force winds delayed the carrier's sailing for 24 hours. She eventually left Glasgow during the afternoon of 17 September.

The voyage to Port Said was uneventful, with the car for the Chief Justice being unloaded in Gibraltar Bay. After stores and equipment had been disembarked at Marsaxlokk Bay, Malta, *Glory* arrived in Port Said during the afternoon of 28 September. Eight hours later, at 2338, she entered the Suez Canal and all went well for the first part of her southbound transit. During the forenoon of 29 September she anchored in the Great Bitter Lake where cargo for the troops in the

Suez Canal Zone was unloaded into lighters. Finally, at 1210 on Thursday 30 September she re-entered the Suez Canal on her voyage south. Less than 30 minutes later, at 1227, the carrier grounded in mud. With silt, sand and mud clogging the seawater circulating system which cooled the main engines, the ship was stopped with no power to her main machinery. That afternoon four tugs struggled to free her and at 1800, in an attempt to lighten the weight aft, all hands who were off watch were ordered to muster on the quarter-deck, and fuel was pumped out into lighters. Finally, at 2055, after eight hours aground, *Glory* was refloated and tugs towed her back into the Great Bitter Lake where she was anchored. Next morning, at 0500, all the ship's divers were mustered to carry out a thorough examination of the hull, rudders and propellers. Meanwhile, down below in the engine rooms, the engineers laboured hard to clear the mud and silt from the circulating system. By 1320 *Glory* was able to weigh anchor and resume her voyage to the east.

There was a short stop of just 12 hours at Aden to disembark cargo and to refuel, and a much more pleasant three-day visit to Trincomalee, where more cargo was unloaded. *Glory* eventually arrived alongside No 8 berth of Singapore Naval Base on 20 October. Once alongside all the helicopters, the remaining passengers and the cargo of trucks were disembarked and a deck cargo of Sea Hawks was embarked for the return passage. The aircraft were

being returned to the UK because there were not enough trained pilots for them in the Far East. For a while at least *Glory's* flight deck looked as busy at it had been during the Korean War. Finally, after embarking Army personnel, most of whom were time-expired national servicemen, *Glory* left Singapore to begin her passage home, via Colombo, Aden and Suez. Her northbound transit of the Suez Canal was completed without incident at 2300 on 18 November and after short stops at Malta (where she embarked more Army personnel and Royal Marines) and Gibraltar, *Glory* arrived back in Portsmouth on Monday 6 December, where all her passengers were disembarked.

With Christmas and New Year spent at Portsmouth, the winter weather in Scotland took a hand in prolonging the carrier's operational career by just over a week. In mid-January 1955 severe snowstorms hit Scotland, and after eight days of heavy blizzards many isolated villages north of Oban were completely cut off, with some areas taking on the appearance of the Arctic. Snowdrifts ten feet deep made it impossible for road and rail traffic to get to many communities, and it was clear that essential supplies would have to be supplied by air. Initially the RAF set up a centre at Wick, from where they could call upon a special fleet of aircraft at Kinloss to undertake emergency work. Also at Wick two Royal Navy Whirlwind helicopters operated from the local airport, being supplied

The ship's cat carrying one of her kittens.

Personnel of the Whirlwind Flight who used *Glory* as a base during the severe winter of January 1954, when many parts of northern Scotland were cut off and supplies had to be dropped from the air.

with fuel by the destroyer *Urchin*, which anchored in Wicks Bay. Meanwhile, *Glory* had steamed north from Portsmouth to Glasgow in order to unload her cargo of Sea Hawks. She was in an ideal position to assist with "Operation Snowdrop", the delivery of food, animal fodder and medical supplies to areas which were cut off. In some cases the helicopters evacuated sick people who required medical attention. On 18 January *Glory* left the Clyde and steamed north to Loch Eriboll on Scotland's north coast, where she anchored to provide a co-ordination and refuelling centre for the naval helicopters operating from Wick. On 19 January the two Whirlwinds dropped 3,300lb of food, kerosene, mail and cattle fodder to 34 villages. Fortunately, after a week of intensive flying operations, more permanent supply routes were being organized. *Glory* continued her passage round Scotland's north coast to arrive in Rosyth Dockyard in the last week of January, where she was secured in the main basin to begin a refit before being placed in reserve. At 1200 on Tuesday 22 February, with the ship having been taken over by the dockyard, Captain

Sims-Williams relinquished command and, with the rest of the ship's company, he moved into *HMS Cochrane*, the RN barracks at Rosyth.

At 1100 on Thursday 5 April 1956, after 14 months in dockyard hands, during which time the whole ship was given a complete overhaul, *Glory* was recommissioned at Rosyth for sea trials, with a much-reduced ship's company. Five days later Captain T. N. Masterman OBE RN, arrived to take command and by the weekend of 5 May the ship was ready for sea. After a 24-hour delay due to bad weather, at 1300 on 8 May *Glory* was manoeuvred out of Rosyth Dockyard basin and she set sail to carry out full-power trials. On Friday 11 May she left the Firth of Forth to set course down the North Sea for Devonport. She arrived three days later and secured to a buoy in the Hamoaze. On Monday 4 June the C-in-C Plymouth visited the ship. Seven days later she left harbour to carry out speed trials, before setting course for the Bristol Channel, where she embarked observers for an air traffic control exercise. During the exercise two Whirlwind helicopters used *Glory* as their base. After disembarking the visitors later in the day she set course for Rosyth, via the Pentland Firth. During the forenoon of Thursday 14 June *Glory* met the newer light fleet carrier *Bulwark*, and that afternoon Captain Masterman was able to visit her by helicopter. During the morning of Friday 15 June *Glory* arrived back at Rosyth, and by 0815 had been secured to a berth in the dockyard's main basin. She had completed her final voyage under her own steam, and at 1200 on Friday 22 June 1956 she was finally paid off.

Glory remained in reserve at Rosyth until, in 1957, having been joined on the disposal list by her sisters *Ocean* and *Theseus*, she was put up for sale. There were rumours about her eventual fate, and there was even a question tabled in Parliament as to whether she might be used as a troop transport.

Glory lay moored and rusting in the Firth of Forth for the best part of five years, but finally, in August 1961, she was towed the short distance to Inverkeithing where she was broken up. For an aircraft carrier which had been designed to last for the duration of the Second World War, she had seen an operational career of 11 years, and made the largest single contribution of any British aircraft carrier to United Nations operations during the Korean War.

Appendix One

Principal Particulars

Dimensions:

Length oa:	695ft
Beam:	112ft - 6in

Tonnage:

Standard Displacement:	13,190
Deep Displacement:	18,040
Draught:	23ft - 5in

Armament:

Defensive Armament:	Four quadruple 2pdr pom-pom. 16 single 40mm Bofors.
Aircraft:	42

Main Propulsion Machinery: Twin screw. Two sets of Parsons geared steam turbines in two engine rooms. Four Admiralty Three-Drum boilers in two boiler rooms. 40,000 SHP. Speed 25 knots.

Complement: 1,300.

Miscellaneous Information:

Aircraft Lifts: Forward and aft 45ft x 34ft wide.

Catapult: One BH3 hydraulic twin-track. 16,000lb, 66 knots.

Pennant Number: R62

Deck Recognition Letters: L, Y and R.

Appendix Two

Commanding Officers

Name	Date of Appointment
Captain Sir A. W. Buzzard OBE DSO RN	1 November 1944
Captain W. D. Couchman DSO OBE RN	6 September 1946
Captain E. H. Shattock OBE RN	15 August 1949
Captain H. Traill CBE RN	27 December 1949
Captain E. H. Shattock OBE RN	12 February 1950
Captain K. S. Colquhoun DSO RN	28 December 1950
Captain T. A. K. Maunsell RN	23 April 1952
Acting Captain D. E. Bromley-Martin RN	30 November 1952
Captain E. D. G. Lewin DSO DSC* RN	14 December 1952
Captain R. T. White DSO** RN	3 September 1953
Captain H. W. S. Sims-Williams RN	7 July 1954
Captain T. N. Masterman RN	10 April 1956

Battle Honours

Per Concordiam Gloria
(Glory through Unity)

The Glorious First of June 1794

Martinique 1809

Guadeloupe 1810

Dardanelles 1915

Korea 1951-53

Former *Glorys*

The first ship of the name actually started her career as the French ship *Gloire*, but she was captured as a prize in 1747. She was a Fifth Rate of some 748 tons and armed with 44 guns. At one stage in her career her commanding officer was Lord Howe. In 1757 she was reduced to 30 guns and in 1763 she was sold.

Another *Glory* was built in 1763 and she was a Third Rate of 679 tons, armed with 32 guns. In 1774 she was renamed *Apollo*, and she was broken up in 1786.

In 1788 a Second Rate of 1,931 tons, armed with 98 guns was named *Glory*. Between 28 May and 1 June 1794 *Glory* formed part of Admiral Lord Howe's fleet which participated in The Glorious First of June, a battle which took place in the North Atlantic, with the French fleet of Admiral Villaret-Joyeuse It was the first major encounter at sea between the warring countries. The outcome, despite the name given to the battle, was not easy to assess, although on the face of it Howe triumphed. The battle was the culmination of weeks of patient patrolling in the Western Approaches by Howeís fleet of 34 of the line. Their reward came on 28 May when Howe's flagship, *Queen Charlotte*, sighted Joyeuse's 28 ships of the line. In February 1809 she was part of Admiral Sir Alexander Cochrane's force which helped capture the island of Martinique. In February 1810, still part of Cochrane's fleet, she assisted with the capture of the island of Guadeloupe, thereby gaining the third battle honour. *Glory* was scrapped in 1825.

The next three ships were all named *La Gloire* and were French prizes, which served the Royal Navy under their original name. They were Fifth Rates of 877 tons, 1,153 tons and 1,066 tons respectively, the last one being sold at Devonport in 1817.

In March 1899, the third Canapus-class battleship to be launched was named *Glory*. She served with the Channel Fleet until October 1906, when she was placed in Commissioned Reserve at Portsmouth. Between March and July 1907 she was refitted and equipped with fire control, and magazine cooling and her machinery was overhauled before being recommissioned. In 1909 she served with the Mediterranean Fleet, before being reduced to reserve. In August 1914 she joined the 8th Battle Squadron and carried out convoy duties, as well as acting as the flagship on the West Indies Station. In 1915 she was transferred to the Mediterranean where, with her sisters *Albion* and *Ocean*, she took part in the ill-fated Dardanelles campaign. In 1916 she acted as guardship at Archangel for three years, before moving to Rosyth where, in 1920, she was renamed *Crescent*. In 1922 she was sold for breaking up.

On 14 July 1918, at Archangel, with Britain having become involved in the Russian civil war, the cruiser *Askold*, which was under Bolshevik control, was seized by the Royal Navy. She was renamed *Glory IV* and saw service in the White Sea, before being laid up at Gareloch in 1919. In 1921 she was returned to the Russians and in the following year she was scrapped in Germany.

Roll of Honour

The following men of the Fleet Air Arm made the ultimate sacrifice whilst serving in *HMS Glory*.

Adams JF	Air Mechanic (Engines) 2	27 September 1946
Barrett RE	Lieutenant	25 December 1952
Bates GH	Lieutenant Commander MBE	7 March 1947
Berry E	Leading Airman	8 February 1946
Bettell JWF	Lieutenant	6 October 1950
Boore WH	Sub Lieutenant (Air)	26 April 1946
Bradbrook FG	Commissioned Air Engineer	21 November 1953
Bradley RD	Sub Lieutenant	14 February 1953
Brigstocke TO	Lieutenant	4 January 1950
Colman VV	Petty Officer (Air)	19 November 1952
Cotton WE	Lieutenant Commander	25 October 1951
Daniels AP	Lieutenant DSM	16 December 1952
Davey RGA	Sub Lieutenant	22 September 1951
Dooley AC	Sub Lieutenant (Air)	13 January 1946
Duffy PJ	Sub Lieutenant (Air)	7 February 1946
Fogden PG	Lieutenant	20 December 1952
Ford SWE	Pilot 3rd Class	5 June 1951
Green WH	Naval Airman (1)	21 July 1946
Harris PEM	Lieutenant	27 September 1950
Keates WJB	Sub Lieutenant	25 April 1953
Lawson JAB	Lieutenant (Air)	18 June 1946
MacKinnon DS	Lieutenant	4 March 1947
MacPherson CA	Lieutenant	11 February 1953
Mayne DE	Lieutenant	7 March 1947
Mills P	Sub Lieutenant (Air)	15 December 1945
Mudford JDF	Lieutenant	24 May 1950
Neville-Jones R	Lieutenant	18 November 1952
Overton RJ	Lieutenant	15 March 1952
Rayner BE	Sub Lieutenant	5 January 1953
Ripley ER	Aircrewman 1	16 December 1952
Ryan WG	Leading Airman	16 April 1945
Sadler T	Air Mechanic (Airframes) 1	20 July 1947
Sanderson PAD	Sub Lieutenant (Air)	22 January 1946
Sharp JH	Lieutenant	28 June 1951
Shepley IR	Sub Lieutenant	16 July 1951
Simonds JM	Sub Lieutenant (Air)	5 January 1953
Snape AM	Sub Lieutenant (Air)	16 April 1945
Sparke TW	Commissioned Pilot	18 July 1951
Stephenson EPL	Lieutenant	28 April 1951
Thurstan RP	Lieutenant Commander	29 April 1947
Turney AWR	Lieutenant	4 Janauary 1950
Ward RJ	Lieutenant DSC	22 March 1950
Wells GB	Aircrewman 1 DSM M-i-D*	28 June 1951
Williams R	Lieutenant	16 July 1951
Williams TJ	Naval Airman (1)	27 December 1951

A Sea Fury makes a bad landing, drops a wing and...

...goes over the starboard side aft of the island...

....hits the water, turns over, and...

...begins to sink, but fortunately, the pilot clears his plane and the planeguard destroyer moves in to rescue him.

Acknowledgements

I would like to thank my wife Freda and daughter Louise for their help and support, and their seemingly endless proof reading.

Special thanks should also go to the staff of Fleet Air Arm Museum from whose archives all of the photographs were sourced, in particular to David O'Brien who produced high quality prints from the original photographs; David Hobbs, Jerry Shore, Catherine Rounsfell and Jan Keohane who all fielded numerous requests for additional material and verification of detail.

Neil McCart

The Fleet Air Arm Museum Archive has a collection of records that cover all aspects of British naval aviation, from the Royal Naval Air Service to the modern Fleet Air Arm. Aircraft, ships, equipment, air stations, operations and personnel are all covered. The Museum's Centre for Naval Aviation Records and Research assists hundreds of enquiries each year. Amongst the most regularly consulted are the Squadron Line Books and Record Books, Air Publications and aircraft accident records. The very large photograph collection covers all areas within the Museum's remit and is used widely by researchers and authors.

Anyone who wishes to consult the Fleet Air Arm Museum archive should contact the Centre for Naval Aviation Records and Research at the Fleet Air Arm Museum, Box D6, RNAS Yeovilton, Ilchester, Somerset, BA22 8HT.